Key Stage 3

Mathematics

Author
Fiona C Mapp

Series editor
Alan Brewerton

Revision Notes

Letts
EDUCATIONAL

Every effort has been made to trace copyright holders and to obtain their permission for the use of copyright material. The authors and publishers will gladly receive information enabling them to rectify any error or omission in subsequent editions.

First published 1998

Letts Educational, Schools and Colleges Division, 9–15 Aldine Street, London W12 8AW
Tel. 0181 740 2270
Fax 0181 740 2280

Text © Fiona C Mapp 1998

Editorial, design and production by Hart McLeod, Cambridge

British Library Cataloguing-in-Publication Data
A CIP record for this book is available from the British Library

ISBN 1 84085 034 5

Printed and bound in Great Britain by Ashford Colour Press, Gosport

Letts Educational is the trading name of BPP (Letts Educational) Ltd

Acknowledgements
The author and publishers are grateful to the staff at Cottenham Village College, Cambridge, for their technical assistance.

Contents

Preparing for your Key Stage 3 SATs

You may remember taking National Tests (often called SATs) in Science, English and Maths when you were about 7 and 11 years old. Your Key Stage 3 SATs, taken in May at the end of Year 9, are the last National Tests that you will take before your GCSE examinations in two years' time.

The Key Stage 3 SATs are important because they help show how much you have improved in these three important subjects. They will also help you, your parents and your teachers plan ahead for your GCSE courses next year. Your teachers may use the results of your SATs to help place you in the most appropriate teaching group for some of your GCSE courses.

It is, therefore, a good idea to be well prepared when you take your SATs. Good preparation will lead to good marks and increased confidence. This is where this book is of value.

How to use this book

This book will help you prepare for your SATs in the easiest possible way. It is clearly divided into National Curriculum topics which you will have covered during the past three years. The information is presented as a series of facts, explanations and examples which will help to refresh your memory and improve your understanding.

The book also contains useful tips and advice from examiners which show you how to avoid common mistakes and improve your marks. There is also space for you to make your own notes and comments. Each section finishes with a short test so that you can check that you have covered the topic sufficiently.

You will see the label 'For Level 7 only' from time to time. The sections indicated are for those students taking Level 7 and above; ask your teacher if you are unsure about the levels you are taking in your SATs.

Your SATs are important, and this book gives you an excellent opportunity of making the most of them.

 Good luck

Number and algebra

Directed numbers

Examiner's
tips and
your notes

- These are numbers which may be **positive** or **negative**. Positive are above zero, negative are below zero.

- Negative numbers are commonly used to describe temperatures, i.e. −3 °C means 3 °C below zero.

Examples

−4 is smaller than 4.

−2 is bigger than −5.

Example

Arrange these temperatures in order of size, smallest first.
−6 °C, 4 °C, −10 °C, 3 °C, 2 °C, −1 °C

Arranged in order: −10 °C, −6 °C, −1 °C, 2 °C, 3 °C, 4 °C.

Adding and subtracting directed numbers

- When adding and subtracting directed numbers it is helpful to draw a number line.

Example

The temperature at 3 p.m. was 2 °C; by 11 p.m. it had dropped by 7 °C. What is the temperature at 11 p.m.?

Drawing
a number
line often
helps.

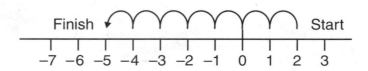

The new temperature is −5 °C.

Note the different uses of the minus signs.

Example

Find the value of −2 − 7 (note the different uses of the minus sign).

$$-2 - 7$$

This represents the sign of the number, i.e. start at −2.

This represents the operation of subtraction, i.e. Move 7 places to the left.

Finish ← Start
−9 −8 −7 −6 −5 −4 −3 −2 −1 0

- When the number to be added (or subtracted) is negative the normal direction of movement is reversed.

Example

−6 − (−1) is the same as −6 + 1 = −5.

The negative changes the direction.

Move 1 place to the right.

- When two (+) signs or two (−) signs are together then these rules are used:

Care needs to be taken with these types of questions as they can be difficult.

$+(+) = +$ ⎫ **Like** signs give
$-(-) = +$ ⎭ a **positive**.

$+(-) = -$ ⎫ **Unlike** signs give
$-(+) = -$ ⎭ a **negative**.

Examples

$$-2 + (-3) = -2 - 3 = -5 \qquad -4 - (+4) = -4 - 4 = -8$$
$$5 - (-2) = 5 + 2 = 7 \qquad 6 + (-2) = 6 - 2 = 4$$

For Level 7 only

Multiplying and dividing directed numbers

- Multiply and divide the numbers as normal.
- Find the sign for the answer using these rules:

  two **like** signs (both + or both −) give **positive**,

  two **unlike** signs (one + and the other −) give **negative**.

Multiply or divide as normal then put in the sign.

Examples

$$-6 \times (+4) = -24 \qquad -3 \times (-4) = 12$$
$$-24 \div (-2) = 12 \qquad 15 \div (-3) = -5$$

Negative numbers on the calculator

The +/– or (–) key on the calculator gives a negative number.

For example, to get –2, press 2 +/– or (–) 2.

This represents the sign.

Example

–6 – (–3) = –3
is keyed into the calculator like this:

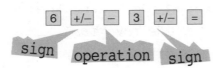

6 +/– – 3 +/– =

sign   operation   sign

Check that you know how to enter it on your calculator.

Fractions

If the numerator and the denominator are the same then it is a whole one, i.e. $\frac{6}{6} = 1$

- A fraction is part of a whole one. $\frac{2}{5}$ means 2 parts out of 5.

- The top number is the **numerator**, the bottom one is the **denominator**.

- A fraction like $\frac{2}{5}$ is called a **proper fraction**.

- A fraction like $\frac{12}{7}$ is called an **improper fraction**.

- A fraction like $1\frac{4}{9}$ is called a **mixed number**.

Equivalent fractions

- These are fractions which have the same value.

Example

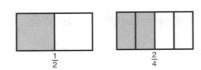

$\frac{1}{2}$ $\frac{2}{4}$

From the diagram it can be seen that:

$$\frac{1}{2} = \frac{2}{4}$$

- Fractions can be changed into their equivalent by either **multiplying** or **dividing** the numerator and denominator by the same amount.

Examples

$$\frac{7}{9} = \frac{?}{27}$$

$$\frac{35}{50} = \frac{7}{?}$$

This method can be used to simplify fractions.

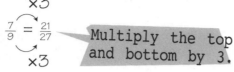

$$\overset{\times 3}{\underset{\times 3}{\frac{7}{9} = \frac{21}{27}}}$$

Multiply the top and bottom by 3.

$$\overset{\div 5}{\underset{\div 5}{\frac{35}{50} = \frac{7}{10}}}$$

Divide the top and bottom by 5.

Using the fraction key on the calculator

$\boxed{a^{b}/_{c}}$ is the fraction key on the calculator.

Example

$\frac{20}{30}$ is keyed in as $\boxed{2}$ $\boxed{0}$ $\boxed{a^{b}/_{c}}$ $\boxed{3}$ $\boxed{0}$.

This is displayed as $\boxed{20 \lrcorner 30}$ or $\boxed{20 \ulcorner 30}$.

The calculator will automatically cancel down fractions when the $\boxed{=}$ key is pressed. For example, $\frac{20}{30}$ becomes $\boxed{2 \lrcorner 3}$ or $\boxed{2 \ulcorner 3}$.

This means two-thirds.

Check: your calculator may have a $\boxed{\text{2nd}}$ or $\boxed{\text{Inv}}$ key instead of $\boxed{\text{Shift}}$.

A display of $\boxed{1 \lrcorner 5 \lrcorner 7}$ means $1\frac{5}{7}$. If you now press $\boxed{\text{shift}}$ $\boxed{a^{b}/_{c}}$, it converts back to an improper fraction, $\boxed{12 \lrcorner 7}$.

Decimals

- A decimal point is used to separate whole number columns from fractional columns.

Example

Thousands	Hundreds	Tens	Units	Tenths	Hundredths	Thousandths
6	7	1	4 .	2	3	8

decimal point

- The 2 means 2/10.

- The 3 means 3/100.

- The 8 means 8/1000.

Remember, hundredths are smaller than tenths, i.e. $\frac{3}{100}$ is smaller than $\frac{2}{10}$.

Recurring decimals

- A decimal that **recurs** is shown by placing a dot over the numbers that repeat.

Examples

$0.66666\ldots = 0.\dot{6}$ $0.147147\ldots = 0.\dot{1}4\dot{7}$

Ordering decimals

When ordering decimals:

- First write them with the same number of figures after the decimal point.

- Then compare whole numbers, digits in the tenths place, digits in the hundredths place, and so on.

Example

Arrange these numbers in order of size, smallest first:

4.27, 4.041, 4.7, 6.4, 2.19, 4.72.

First rewrite them:

4.270, 4.041, 4.700, 6.400, 2.190, 4.720.

Then reorder them:

2.190   4.041   4.270   4.700   4.720   6.400.

Have a quick check that all values are included.

the zero is smaller than the two.

Rounding numbers

Decimal places (d.p.)

When rounding to a specified number of decimal places:

- Look at the last digit that is wanted (if rounding 8.347 to 2 d.p. look at the 4 (second decimal place).

- Look at the number next to it (look at the number not needed, i.e. the 7).

- If it is **5 or more** round up the last digit (7 is greater than 5, so round the 4 up to a 5).

- If it is **less than 5**, the digit remains the **same**.

Examples

16.5**9** = 16.6 to 1 d.p.

8.4**35** = 8.44 to 2 d.p.

12.3**4** = 12.3 to 1 d.p.

For
Level 7
only

Significant figures (s.f. or sig. fig.)

Apply the same rule as with decimal places. If the next digit is 5 or more round up. The first significant figure is the first digit which is not a zero. The 2nd, 3rd, 4th, . . . significant figures follow on after the first digit. They may or may not be zeros.

Examples

7.021 has 4 s.f.

1st 2nd 3rd 4th

0.003706 has 4 s.f.

1st 2nd 3rd 4th

Take care when rounding that you do not change the place values.

Examples

Number	to 3 s.f.	to 2 s.f.	to 1 s.f.
4.207	4.21	4.2	4
4379	4380	4400	4000
0.006 209	0.006 21	0.0062	0.006

After rounding you must fill in the end zeros. For example, 4380 = 4400 to 2 s.f. (not 44). No extra zeros must be put in after the decimal point. For example, 0.013 = 0.01 to 2 s.f. (not 0.010).

Percentages

These are fractions with a **denominator of 100**. For example 62% $= \frac{62}{100}$.

Equivalences between fractions, decimals and percentages

Fractions, decimals and percentages all mean the same thing but are just written in a different way.

Fraction		Decimal		Percentage
$\frac{1}{4}$	$1 \div 4$	0.25	$\times 100\%$	25%
$\frac{6}{10}$		0.6		60%
$\frac{1}{6}$		0.166$\dot{6}$		16.6$\dot{6}$%

Ordering different numbers

When putting fractions, decimals and percentages in order of size, it is best to change them all to **decimals** first.

Make sure you put the values in the order the question says.

Example

Place in order of size, smallest first:

$\frac{1}{4}$, 0.241, 29%, 64%, $\frac{1}{3}$

0.25, 0.241, 0.29, 0.64, 0.3$\dot{3}$ Put into decimals first.

0.241, 0.25, 0.29, 0.3$\dot{3}$, 0.64 Now order.

Index notation

- An **index** is sometimes known as a **power**.

  6^3 is read as **6 to the power 3**. It means $6 \times 6 \times 6$.

  5^5 is read as **5 to the power 5**. It means $5 \times 5 \times 5 \times 5 \times 5$.

  a^b — known as the **index** or **power**.

  known as the **base**

- The **base** is the value which has to be multiplied. The **index** indicates how many times.

Powers on a calculator display

The value 5×10^6 means $5 \times 10 \times 10 \times 10 \times 10 \times 10 \times 10$

$$= 5\,000\,000.$$

On a calculator display 5×10^6 would look like $\boxed{5 \quad {}^{06}}$.

On a calculator display 7×10^{19} would look like $\boxed{7 \quad {}^{19}}$.

Place value and the number system
Questions

1 The temperature inside the house is 12 °C warmer than outside. If the temperature outside is −5 °C. What is the temperature inside?

2 Work out what the missing letters stand for:

(a) $12 - A = -3$ (b) $-6 + 10 = B$ (c) $-9 \times C = -36$

(d) $-8 - (D) = 2$ (e) $120 \div (E) = -12$ (f) $14 + (F) = -6$

3 Working out the missing values:

(a) $\frac{7}{12} = \frac{14}{x}$ (b) $\frac{125}{500} = \frac{y}{100}$ (c) $\frac{19}{38} = \frac{76}{z}$

4 The weights of some objects are:

2.7 kg, 19.4 kg, 6.032 kg, 6.302 kg, 2.74 kg, 19.04 kg. Arrange the weights in order of size, largest first.

5 Write out fully:

(a) 2^5 (b) 7^3 (c) 8^4

6 Jonathan's calculator display shows, $\boxed{1.52\ ^{06}}$. Write down what the calculator display means.

7 Write 24% as a fraction in its simplest form.

8 A flag is coloured red (27%), blue (61%) and the rest is yellow. What percentage is yellow?

9 Change these fractions into (a) a decimal, (b) a percentage:

(a) $\frac{7}{9}$ (b) $\frac{2}{3}$ (c) $\frac{3}{5}$ (d) $\frac{4}{16}$

10 Round 6.493 to 2 decimal places.

11 Round 12.059 to 2 decimal places.

12 Round 9.47 to 1 decimal place.

13 Round 1247 to 2 significant figures.

14 Round 0.00379 to 1 significant figure.

Relationships between number and computation methods

Using a calculator

Order of operations

Examiner's tips and your notes

Bodmas is a made up word which helps you to remember the order in which calculations take place.

B   o   D   M   A   S

Brackets   over   Division   Multiplication   Addition   Subtraction

This just means that brackets are carried out first then the others are done in order.

Examples

$(2 + 4) \times 3 = 18$

$6 + 2 \times 4 = 14,$ not 32 because multiplication is done first.

Important calculator keys

Practise on your own calculator and check you know how to use these keys.

(–) or +/– Change positive numbers to negative ones.

C This only cancels the last key you have pressed.

AC This cancels all the work.

a^b/c This key allows a fraction to be put in the calculator.

√ Square root button.

x^2 Square button on some calculators.

Shift   2nd   Inv   These allow 2nd functions to be carried out.

Min, MR, M+ These are memory keys.

For Level 7 only

[(...., ...)] These are brackets keys.

When calculating complex fractions use either the brackets keys or memory keys.

Example

$$\frac{1.4 \times \sqrt{27}}{6.4 + 9.3} = 0.46 \ (2 \ d.p.)$$

Check that you obtain this answer on your calculator.

Estimates and approximations

- A good way of checking answers is by estimating. Numbers are usually rounded to the nearest 10/100/1000, etc.

Example

A tin of cat food weighs 58 g; estimate the weight of 306 tins.

$$58 \times 306 \approx 60 \times 300 = 18\,000$$

- ≈ means approximately equal to.

A quick way of multiplying 60×300 is $6 \times 3 = 18$, then place 3 zeros on the end, 18 000.

Types of number

Multiples

These are just the numbers in multiplication tables. For example, multiples of 6 are 6, 12, 18, 24, . . .

Factors

These are whole numbers which divide exactly into other numbers. For example, factors of 12 are 1, 2, 3, 4, 6, 12.

Prime numbers

Make sure you know the prime numbers up to 20.

These are numbers which only have 2 factors, **1 and itself**. Prime numbers up to 20 are

2, 3, 5, 7, 11, 13, 17, 19.

Note that 1 is not a prime number.

For Level 7 only

Prime factors

These are factors which are prime.

Some numbers can be written as a product of their prime factors.

Example

The diagram shows the prime factors of 50.

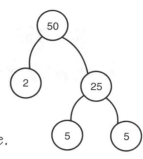

- Divide 50 by its first prime factor 2.

- Divide 25 by its first prime factor 5.

- Keep on going until the final number is prime.

As a product of its prime factors, 50 may be written as:

Remember to write the final answer as a multiplication.

$2 \times 5 \times 5 = 50$

or $2 \times 5^2 = 50$

in **index** notation (using powers).

Squares and cubes

- Anything to the **power 2** is **square**. For example, $3^2 = 3 \times 3 = 9$.

- Anything to the **power 3** is **cube**. For example, $4^3 = 4 \times 4 \times 4 = 64$.

Square numbers include:

1
1×1

4
2×2

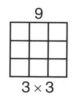
9
3×3

16
4×4

Cube numbers include:

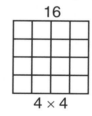
1
$1 \times 1 \times 1$

8
$2 \times 2 \times 2$

27
$3 \times 3 \times 3$

Square and cube numbers can be represented by a diagram.

Square roots and cube roots

$\sqrt{}$ is the **square root sign**. Taking the square root is the opposite of squaring, for example, $\sqrt{36} = 6$ since $6 \times 6 = 36$.

$\sqrt[3]{}$ is the **cube root sign**. Taking the cube root is the opposite of cubing, for example, $\sqrt[3]{64} = 4$ since $4 \times 4 \times 4 = 64$.

Multiplying and dividing by numbers between 0 and 1

- When **multiplying** by numbers between 0 and 1, the result is **smaller** than the starting value.

- When **dividing** by numbers between 0 and 1, the result is **bigger** than the starting value.

Examples

$4 \times 0.1 = 0.4$ $4 \div 0.1 = 40$

$4 \times 0.01 = 0.04$ $4 \div 0.01 = 400$

$4 \times 0.001 = 0.004$ $4 \div 0.001 = 4000$

The result is **smaller** than the starting value.

The result is **bigger** than the starting value.

Long multiplication

Example

A single plant costs 42p. Without a calculator work out the cost of 164 plants.

```
  164
   42 ×
 ─────
  328        Step 1: 164 x 2
 6560 +      Step 2: 164 x 40
 ─────
 6888        Step 3: 328 + 6560.
Cost = 6888p or £68.88.
```

42p each

Make your working out clear.

Long division

Example

A vase costs 74p. Tracey has £9.82 to spend. What is the maximum number of vases Tracey can buy? How much change does she have left? Do this calculation without using a calculator.

Remember to change the units first.

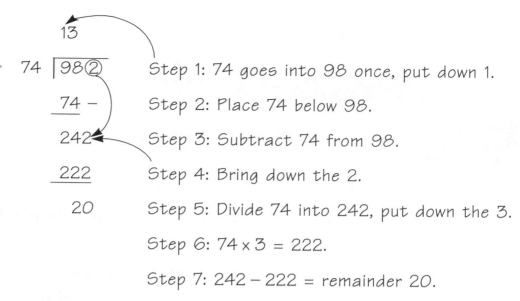

```
        13
74 | 98 ②
     74 –
     242
    _222_
      20
```

Step 1: 74 goes into 98 once, put down 1.

Step 2: Place 74 below 98.

Step 3: Subtract 74 from 98.

Step 4: Bring down the 2.

Step 5: Divide 74 into 242, put down the 3.

Step 6: 74 x 3 = 222.

Step 7: 242 – 222 = remainder 20.

Tracey can buy 13 vases and has 20p left over.

Calculations with decimals

Examples

When adding or subtracting decimals make sure they have the same number of place values, i.e. 4.9 = 4.90.

Add together 6.21 and 4.9.

```
  6.21
  4.90
 _11.11_
```

Put the decimal points under each other.

This is the same as 4.9

The decimal point in the answer will be in line.

Subtract 6.2 from 12.81.

```
  12.81
   6.20 –
  _6.61_
```

The decimal points are in line.

```
  12.3
    7 x
  861
```

Multiply 123 by 7 = 861, ignore the decimal point.

Since 12.3 has 1 number after the decimal point then so must the answer.

Answer = 86.1.

```
       4.3
  6 | 25.8
```

When dividing, divide as normal, placing the decimal points in line.

Put the decimal points in line.

Fractions

Fractions of a quantity

Examiner's tips and your notes

- The word **of** means **multiply**.

Example

In a class of 40 students $\frac{2}{5}$ of them are left-handed. How many are left-handed?

$\frac{2}{5}$ of 40 means $\frac{2}{5} \times 40 = 16$ students.

On the calculator key in

| 2 | ÷ | 5 | × | 40 | = |

This can be worked out by dividing 40 by 5 to find $\frac{1}{5}$ and then multiply by 2 to find $\frac{2}{5}$.

Percentages

Percentage of a quantity

- The word **of** means **multiply**.

Replace the word **of** with a × sign. Rewrite the percentage as a fraction.

Example

Find 15% of £650.

$\frac{15}{100} \times 650 = £97.50$.

On the calculator key in

| 15 | ÷ | 100 | × | 650 | = |

- If working out mentally, find 10% = 650 ÷ 10 = £65. 5% is half of £65 = £32.50. Add the two together to give £97.50.

One quantity as a percentage of another

- To make the answer a **percentage** multiply by **100%**.

Example

A survey shows that 26 people out of 45 preferred 'Supersuds' washing powder. What percentage preferred Supersuds?

$\frac{26}{45} \times 100\% = 57.\dot{7}\%$ (1 d.p.)

On the calculator key in

| 26 | ÷ | 45 | × | 100 | = |

Make a fraction with the two numbers. Multiply by 100% to get a percentage.

Proportional changes with fractions and percentages

- Fractions and percentages often appear in real life problems.

Examples

The table shows some information about pupils in a school.

	Not vegetarian	Vegetarian
Girls	147	62
Boys	183	41

There are 433 pupils in the school, (147 + 62 + 183 + 41).

(a) What fraction are vegetarian?

(b) What percentage of the pupils are boys?

Always check that your answers sound reasonable.

(a) Vegetarian = 62 + 41 = 103

Fraction $= \frac{103}{433}$

(b) Percentage of boys: $\frac{224}{433} \times 100\% = 51.7 = 52\%$.

Example

BEANOZ

225 g

The tin of baked beans holds 225 g. During a sales promotion 12% extra is added. How many grams of beans are now in the tin?

$\frac{12}{100} \times 225 = 27$ g   Work out 12% increase.

New amount of beans is 225 + 27 = 252 g.

Add the increase onto the original weight.

Repeated percentage change

Show your
working
clearly.
Make sure
these
problems
are worked
out step by
step.

Example

A clothing shop has a sale. For each day of the sale, prices were reduced by 20% of the prices on the day before. A jumper had a price of £45 on Monday. If the sale starts on Tuesday how much would Mary pay for the jumper if she bought it on Wednesday?

Monday price = £45.

Tuesday reduction = $\frac{20}{100} \times 45 = £9$.

New price = £45 − £9 = £36.

Wednesday reduction = $\frac{20}{100} \times 36 = £7.20$.

New price = £36 − £7.20 = £28.80.

Mary paid £28.80.

Make sure you do not do 2 × 20 = 40% reduction over 2 days.

Ratio

A ratio is used to compare two or more quantities.

- **Compared to** is replaced with **two dots** :

Sharing a quantity in a given ratio

- Add up the total parts.
- Work out what one part is worth.
- Work out what the other parts are worth.

Example

A quick check
is by working
out the number
of acres the
oak trees
cover. The
total of the
oak + ash should
be equal to
25 000 acres.

A forest covers 25 000 acres. Oak and ash trees are planted in the forest in the ratio 2 : 3. How many acres do the ash trees cover?

2 + 3 = 5 parts.

5 parts = 25 000 acres.

1 part = $\frac{25\,000}{5}$ = 5000 acres.

Ash has 3 parts, i.e. 3 × 5000 = 15 000 acres.

For
Level 7
only

Increasing and decreasing in a given ratio

- Divide to get one part.

- Multiply for each new part.

Example

A recipe for 6 people needs 420 g of flour. How much is needed for 8 people?

- Divide 420 g by 6 = 70 g for 1 person.

- Multiply by 8 = 70 x 8 = 560 g for 8 people.

Example

A photocopier is set to reduce in the ratio of 3 : 5. What is the length of the reduced diagram if the original is 12 cm?

- Divide 12 by 5 to get 1 part = 2.4 cm.

- Multiply this by 3 to get 3 x 2.4 = 7.2 cm.

Relationships between number and computation methods

Questions

1 Without a calculator work out:

    (a) $4 \times (2 + 3)$ (b) $6 + 4 \times 5$

2 Work out the following:

    (a) $\dfrac{6.2 + (4.6)^2}{\sqrt{3.2} \times 1.7}$ (b) $\dfrac{\sqrt{9.4} - 2.7}{6.1 + 8.2}$

3 1 2 3 4

    5 6 7 8

    9 10 11 12

    From the above numbers write down:

    (a) Any multiples of 3.

    (b) Any prime numbers.

    (c) Factors of 20.

4 Work out the prime factors of 24.

5 Work out without a calculator:

    (a) $\sqrt{100}$ (b) 6^2 (c) $\sqrt{36}$ (d) 2^3

6 Without a calculator work out:

    (a) 6×0.001 (b) 400×0.01 (c) $50 \div 0.001$

7 A tin of soup costs 68p. Work out the cost of 18 tins without using a calculator.

8 The cost of a trip is £10.25. If Mr Appleyard collects in £133.25 how many people are going on the trip? Work out without using a calculator.

9 Out of a class of 31, 12 are left-handed. What percentage are left-handed?

10 A jumper costs £30. If it is reduced in the sale by 15%, how much does it now cost?

11 5/8 of a class of 24 walk to school. How many pupils walk to school?

12 Ahmed and Fiona share £500 between them in the ratio 2 : 3. How much does each receive?

13 A recipe for 12 people uses 500 g of plain flour. How much flour is needed for 18 people?

Solving numerical problems

Calculations

- When solving problems the answers should be rounded sensibly.

Example

$12.1 \times 4.6 = 55.66 = 55.7$ (1 d.p.)

Round to 1 d.p. since the values in the questions are to 1 d.p.

Example

James has £15.36. He divides it equally between 5 people. How much does each person receive?

$£15.36 \div 5 = £3.072$
$ = £3.07.$

Round to £3.07 since it is money.

Interpreting the calculator display

Don't forget to put the zero on the end, i.e. £6.7 is £6.70.

- When questions involve money the following points need to be remembered:

  a display of $\boxed{6.7}$ means £6.70 (Six pounds seventy pence),

  a display of $\boxed{5.03}$ means £5.03 (Five pounds and three pence),

  a display of $\boxed{0.82}$ means £0.82 or 82 pence,

  a display of $\boxed{6.2934}$ needs to be rounded to 2 d.p., i.e. £6.29.

Checking calculations

- When checking calculations the process can be reversed like this.

$102 \times 6 = 612.$ Check $612 \div 6 = 102.$

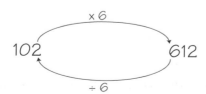

Trial and improvement

- This is when successive approximations are made in order to get closer to the correct value.

Example

If $12x - x^2 = 34$, use trial and improvement to find the value of x to 1 decimal place.

Draw a table to help.

Substitute different values of x into $12x - x^2$.

> Remember x^2 means x times x.

x	$12x - x^2$	Comment
3	$36 - 9 = 27$	too small
4	$48 - 16 = 32$	too small
5	$60 - 25 = 35$	too big
4.5	$54 - 20.25 = 33.75$	too small
4.6	$55.2 - 21.16 = 34.04$	too big
4.55	$54.6 - 20.7025 = 33.8975$	too small

> Remember it is the value of x which is the answer, i.e. 4.6 not 34.04.

At this stage the solution is trapped between 4.5 and 4.6. Checking the middle value x = 4.55 gives $12x - x^2 = 33.8975\ldots$ which is very close to 34.

4.5	4.55	4.6
(too small)	(too small)	(just too big)

The diagram shows that even though 4.6 is slightly too big it is the closest solution to 1 decimal place.

Best buys

- Unit amounts are looked at to decide which is the better value for money.

Example

£1.06   £2.81

The same brand of breakfast cereal is sold in two different sized packets. Which packet represents the better value for money?

- Find the cost per gram for each packet.

  125 g = £1.06   Cost of 1 g = 106 ÷ 125 = 0.848 p.

  750 g = £2.81   Cost of 1 g = 281 ÷ 750 = 0.3746 p.

- Since the 750 g packet costs less per gram, it is the better value for money.

For Level 7 only ▶

Compound measures

Speed can be measured in kilometres per hour (km/h), miles per hour (mph) and metres per second (m/s). Km/h, mph and m/s are all **compound measures**, because they involve a combination of basic measures — in this case distance and time.

Speed

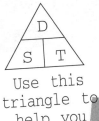

Use this triangle to help you remember the formulae.

Average speed = $\dfrac{\text{Total distance travelled}}{\text{Total time taken}} = \dfrac{D}{T}$

Just remember the letters — it is quicker.

From the speed formula two other formulae can be found.

Time = $\dfrac{\textbf{Distance}}{\textbf{Speed}}$ Distance = **Speed** × **Time**.

Always check the units first, before starting a question and change them if necessary.

Example

Lynette walks 10 km in 4 hours. Find her average speed.

$$S = \frac{D}{T} \quad = \frac{10}{4} \quad = 2.5 \text{ km/h.}$$

The units are km/h since the distance is km and the time is in hours.

Example

Mr Singh drove a distance of 500 miles at an average speed of 70 mph. How long did the journey take?

$$T = \frac{D}{S} \qquad = \frac{500}{70} \qquad = 7.14\ldots \text{hours}.$$

This answer does not mean 7 hrs 14 minutes.

7.14 ... hours must be changed into hours and minutes.

- Subtract the hours 7.14 ... − 7 = 0.14 ... hours.

- Multiply the decimal part by 60 minutes.

$$0.14\ldots \times 60 \qquad = 8.6 \qquad = 9 \text{ minutes to the nearest minute}.$$

Time = 7 hours 9 minutes.

Density

Use this triangle to help you remember the formulae.

Density = $\dfrac{\text{Mass}}{\text{Volume}}$ **Volume = $\dfrac{\text{Mass}}{\text{Density}}$**   **Mass = Density × Volume**

$$D = \frac{M}{V} \qquad\qquad V = \frac{M}{D} \qquad\qquad M = D \times V$$

Example

Find the density of an object whose mass is 600 g and whose volume is 50 cm³.

Remember to put in the units at the end of a question.

$$\text{Density} = \frac{M}{V} \qquad = \frac{600}{50} \qquad = 12 \text{ g/cm}^3.$$

Since the mass is in grams and the volume in cm³, Density is in g/cm³.

Solving numerical problems
Questions

1 Using a calculator work out 6.59×3.87, rounding your answer sensibly.

2 Keith has £65, he shares it equally between 6 people. How much does each receive?

3 Liam tries to work out the answer to $x^2 = 8$ by trial and improvement. What answer will he get to 1 decimal place? (Make up a table to help.)

4 The same brand of tuna fish is sold in two different sized tins. Which tin represents the better value for money?

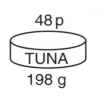
48 p
TUNA
198 g

76 p
TUNA
240 g

5 It takes Diana 30 minutes to walk to the shop 2 km away. At what speed is she travelling?

6 The mass of an object is 500 grams. If the density is 6.2 g/cm³ what is the volume of the object?

7 Bonnie travels to work at a speed of 40 mph. If she works 30 miles away, how long will it take her to get to work?

or
vel
7
lly

Functional relationships

Using letters

- **Algebra** uses letters to represent numbers.

Example

Emily plants a small vegetable garden. She plants potatoes, carrots and onions. *m* stands for the number of carrot seeds she has planted.

If she plants 5 more onion seeds than carrot seeds. How many onion seeds does she plant?

$$m + 5$$

This is known as an **expression**.

If she plants half as many onion seeds as carrot seeds, this is written as

$$m \div 2 \text{ which is usually written as } \frac{m}{2}.$$

Remember that in algebra a division is usually written as a fraction, i.e. $x \div a = \dfrac{x}{a}$.

Example

Richard has *p* counters. David has three times as many counters. Write this as an expression:

David has $3 \times p$ counters.

- $3 \times p$ is written as $3p$ in algebra; the multiplication sign is missed out.

Substitution

- Replacing a letter with a number is called **substitution**. When substituting:

  write out the expression first then replace the letters with the values given,

  work out the value on your calculator. Use brackets keys where possible and pay attention to **order of operations**.

Examples

Using $a = 2$, $b = 4.1$, $c = -3$, $d = 5$, find the value of these expressions, giving your answer to 1 decimal place.

(a) $\dfrac{a+b}{2}$ (b) $\dfrac{a^2+c^2}{d}$ (c) ab (d) $3d - ab$

Show each step in your working out.

Remember to show the substitution:

(a) $\dfrac{a+b}{2} = \dfrac{2+4.1}{2} = 3.05 = 3.1$ (1 d.p.)

> You may need to treat c^2 as $(-3)^2$ depending on your calculator.

(b) $\dfrac{a^2+c^2}{d} = \dfrac{2^2+(-3)^2}{5} = 2.6$

(c) $ab = 2 \times 4.1 = 8.2$

> ab means $a \times b$.

(d) $3d - ab = (3 \times 5) - (2 \times 4.1) = 6.8$.

Number patterns and sequences

A sequence is a list of numbers. There is usually a relationship between the numbers. Each value in the list is called a **term**.

- There are lots of different number patterns. When finding a missing number in the number pattern it is sensible to see what is happening in the gap.

Examples

The odd numbers have **a common difference** of two.

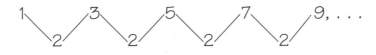

> The rule is add 2 each time.

The next term in this sequence is found by multiplying the previous term by 3.

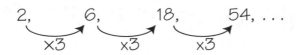

Common number patterns

These number patterns are common and need to be remembered.

1, 4, 9, 16, 25, . . . Square numbers.

1, 8, 27, 64, 125, . . . Cube numbers.

1, 3, 6, 10, 15, . . . Triangular numbers.

1, 1, 2, 3, 5, 8, 13 . . . Fibonacci sequence.

Finding the nth term of a linear sequence

- The nth term is often shown as U_n, e.g. the 12th term is U_{12}.

- For a linear sequence the nth term takes the form of $U_n = an + b$.

Example

Find the nth term of this sequence:

   4, 7, 10, 13, 16.

- Look at the difference between the terms. If they are the same this gives the **multiple** or **a**.

- Adjust the rule by adding or taking away.

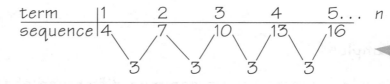

term | 1 | 2 | 3 | 4 | 5... n
sequence | 4 | 7 | 10 | 13 | 16

The gap or difference give the value of a

The multiple is 3, i.e. 3n.

Check your rule with the second term to make sure it works.

If n is 1, $3 \times 1 = 3$ but we need 4 so add 1.

n^{th} term $U_n = 3n + 1.$

Finding the nth term of a quadratic sequence

For a quadratic sequence the first differences are not constant but the second differences are.

The nth term takes the form of $U_n = an^2 + bn + c$, where b and c may be zero.

Example

For the sequence of square numbers find an expression for the nth term.

$$1 \quad\quad 4 \quad\quad 9 \quad\quad 16 \quad\quad 25$$

First difference $\quad 3 \quad\quad 5 \quad\quad 7 \quad\quad 9$

Second difference $\quad\quad 2 \quad\quad 2 \quad\quad 2$

- Since the second differences are the same, the rule for the nth term is quadratic.

- The nth term is n^2.

Coordinates

- Coordinates are used to locate the position of a point.

- When reading coordinates, read across first then up or down.

- Coordinates are always written with **brackets** and a **comma** in between, i.e. $(2, 4)$

- The horizontal axis is the **x** axis. The vertical axis is the **y** axis.

Examples

Remember to read across first then up or down!

A has coordinates $(2, 4)$

B has coordinates $(-1, 3)$

C has coordinates $(-2, -3)$

D has coordinates $(3, -1)$

Make sure you write the brackets and comma.

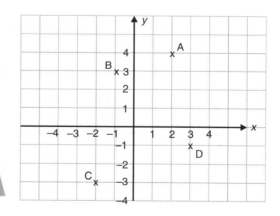

Graph drawing

- Coordinates are used to draw graphs.

- Before a graph can be drawn the coordinates need to be worked out.

Graphs of the form $y = mx + c$

These are straight line (linear) graphs.

The general equation of a straight line graph is **$y = mx + c$**.

m is the **gradient** (steepness) of the line.

c is the **intercept** on the y axis, that is where the graph cuts the y axis.

Parallel lines have the **same gradient**.

Example

Draw the graphs of $y = 2x$, $y = -2x$, $y = 3x$ and $y = x - 2$ on the same axes.

- Work out coordinates for each graph.

> Putting the coordinates in a table makes it easier.

$y = 2x$

x	−2	−1	0	1	2
y	−4	−2	0	2	4

$y = -2x$

x	−2	−1	0	1	2
y	4	2	0	−2	−4

If your line is not straight, go back and check your coordinates.

$y = 3x$

x	−2	−1	0	1	2
y	−6	−3	0	3	6

$y = x - 2$

x	−2	−1	0	1	2
y	−4	−3	−2	−1	0

- Plot each set of coordinates and join up the points with a straight line.

- Label each of the graphs.

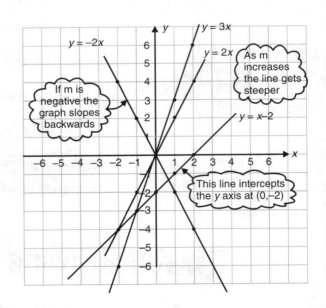

As m increases the line gets steeper

If m is negative the graph slopes backwards

This line intercepts the y axis at (0,−2)

Graphs of the form $y = x^2 + a$

- These are curved graphs.

Example

Use a calculator to help work out the coordinates.

Draw the graph of $y = x^2 - 2$.

x	−3	−2	−1	0	1	2	3
y	7	2	−1	−2	−1	2	7

- Work out the y coordinates for each point.

- Remember that x^2 means x times x.

- Just replace x in the equation with each coordinate, i.e.
  $x = -3$ so $y = -3^2 - 2 = 7$.

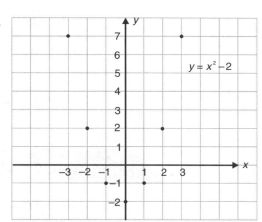

Try and join the points with a smooth curve.

- The table represents the coordinates of the graph. The coordinates can now be plotted to form the graph.

- Join up the points with a smooth curve and label the graph.

Using linear graphs

- Linear graphs are often used to show relationships.

Examples

The graph shows the charges made by a van hire firm.

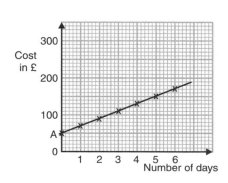

- Point A shows how much was charged for hiring the van, i.e. £50.

- The gradient shows that £20 was then charged per day. Hence for 5 days hire, the van cost £50 + 20 × 5 = £150.

Conversion graphs

- These are used to convert one measurement into another measurement.

When reading off the graph draw on lines to show how you obtained your answers.

Example

£1 = 200 pesetas.

- To change £3.50 into pesetas read up to the line and then across, i.e. 700 pesetas.

- To change 500 pesetas read across to the line and then read down, i.e. £2.50.

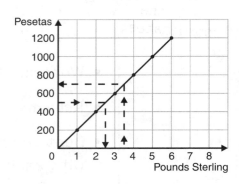

Distance–time graphs

- These are often known as travel graphs. The **speed** of an object can be found from the travel graph.

- From the graph it is seen that the car has travelled 60 km in 2 hours. The speed of the car is 60 ÷ 2 = 30 km/h.

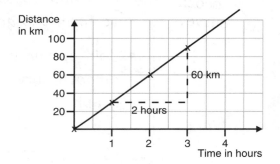

Check the units on the scales.

Functional relationships
Questions

1 Write these expressions as simply as possible.

(a) 6 more than n (b) 4 less than p (c) 6 more than 3 lots of y

(d) h divided by 7   (e) 5 less than n divided by p

2 If $a = 3$, $b = 2.1$, $c = -4$, work out the answer to these expressions giving your answer to 1 d.p.

(a) $3a + 2b$ (b) $5c - 2a$ (c) abc

For level 7 only

3 Find the nth term of this sequence
2, 6, 10, 14, . . .

4 Find the nth term of this sequence
2, 8, 18, 50, . . .

5 What are the coordinates of the
points A, B, C, D, E and F?

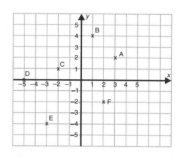

6 The graph of $y = x - 1$ is drawn on the
graph opposite. Draw the following
graphs on the same axes.

(a) $y = 2x$

(b) $y = 4x$

(c) What do you notice about the
graphs of $y = 2x$ and $y = 4x$?

(d) Without working out any
coordinates draw the graph of
$y = x - 2$.

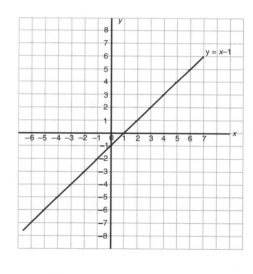

For level 7 only

7 The distance–time graph shows Mrs Roberts'
car journey.

(a) What speed did she travel at for the
first 2 hours?

(b) What is Mrs Roberts doing at A?

(c) At what speed is her return journey?

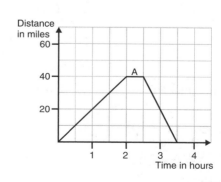

37

Equations and formulae

Algebraic conventions

- There are several rules to follow when writing algebra.

$$a + a + a + a = 4a$$

$$b \times b = b^2 \text{ not } 2b$$

$$b \times b \times b = b^3 \text{ not } 3b$$

$$n \times n \times 3 = 3n^2 \text{ not } (3n)^2$$

$$a \times 3 \times c = 3ac$$

Put the number first and then the letters in alphabetical order; leave out the multiplication sign.

- When dividing, i.e. $a \div 3$, this is usually written as a fraction, i.e. $\frac{a}{3}$.

Writing simple formulae

$n + 4$ is an expression.

$y = n + 4$ is a formula, since it has an = sign in it.

Example

A bag of sweets costs 20p. Erin buys some sweets. How much do

(a) 6 bags cost? (b) 10 bags cost? (c) x bags cost?

(a) $20 \times 6 = 120$ pence.

(b) $20 \times 10 = 200$ pence.

(c) $20 \times x = 20x$ pence.

x can take any value.

In words the above rule can be written as:
Cost of sweets = 20 × number of bags.

This is a **formula** for working out the cost of any number of bags of sweets. If C represents the cost and b represents the number of bags then:

$$C = 20 \times b$$

i.e. $C = 20b$, this formula is in **symbol form**.

Example

The diagrams show some black and white tiles.

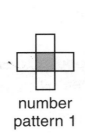

number
pattern 1

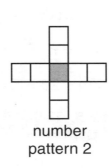

number
pattern 2

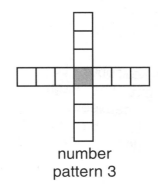

number
pattern 3

(a) How many white tiles will there be in pattern number 4?

Drawing the diagram:

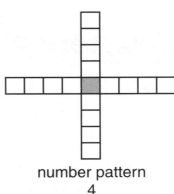

number pattern
4

There are 16 white tiles.

(b) Write down the formula for finding the number of tiles in pattern number n.

> Make sure an = sign is in the formula.

Number of tiles = 4 × n + 1
= $4n + 1$.

> The $4n$ is the 4 lots of white tiles. The +1 is the black tile in the middle.

(c) How many tiles will be used in pattern number 12?

$n = 12$, i.e. number of tiles = 4 × 12 + 1
= 48 + 1
= 49.

> Just substitute the value of n into the formula.

Collecting like terms

- Expressions can be simplified by collecting like terms.

- Only collect the terms if the letters and powers are identical.

Examples

$3p + 2p = 5p.$

$6a + 2c$ cannot be simplified, since there are no like terms.

$5n + 2n - 6n = n$ ◀ Note that n means $1n$.

$2a + 4b + 3a - 2b = 5a + 2b.$ ◀ Add the a's then the b's.

This minus sign is part of the term $2b$.

Remember to put the sign between, i.e. $5a + 2b$ **NOT** $5a$ $2b$.

$5xy + 2yx = 7xy$ since xy is the same as yx.

Multiplying letters and numbers

- Algebraic expressions are often simplified by multiplying them together, i.e. $5a \times 2b = 10ab$.

- When multiplying expressions, multiply the numbers together then the letters together.

Examples

Simplify these expressions:

Multiply the letters

(a) $3a \times 4b = 3 \times 4 \times a \times b = 12ab.$

Multiply the numbers

(b) $5a \times 3b \times 2c = 5 \times 3 \times 2 \times a \times b \times c = 30abc.$

(c) $2a \times 3a = 2 \times 3 \times a \times a = 6a^2.$ ◀ Remember $a \times a = a^2.$

Multiplying out brackets

- This helps to simplify algebraic expressions.

- Multiply everything inside the bracket by everything outside the bracket.

Examples

This is known as **expanding** brackets.

$2(a + b) = 2a + 2b.$

The multiplication sign is not shown here.

$3(x - 2) = 3x - 6.$

Remember $r \times r = r^2$.

$a(b + d) = ab + ad.$

$r(3r - 2s) = 3r^2 - 2rs$

If the term outside the bracket is **negative**, all of the signs of the terms inside the bracket are **changed** when multiplying out.

Examples

Remember that $-(a + b)$ means $-1 \times (a + b)$.

$-2(a + b) = -2a - 2b$

$-a(a - b) = -a^2 + ab$

To simplify expressions, expand the bracket first then collect like terms.

Example

Expand and simplify:

$3(a + 1) + 2(a + b)$ Multiply out brackets.

$3a + 3 + 2a + 2b$ Collect like terms.
$= 5a + 2b + 3.$

Linear equations

- An equation involves an unknown value which has to be worked out.

- The balance method is usually used, that is whatever is done to one side of an equation must be done to the other.

Examples

Solve the following:

Show all working out and do the calculation step by step.

(a) $5n + 1 = 11$

$5n = 11 - 1$ Subtract 1 from both sides.

$5n = 10$

$n = \dfrac{10}{5} = 2.$ Divide both sides by 5.

(b) $\dfrac{n}{3} + 1 = 4$

$\dfrac{n}{3} = 4 - 1$

$\dfrac{n}{3} = 3$ Multiply both sides by 3

$n = 3 \times 3$

$n = 9.$

The answers are not always whole numbers, they can be fractions, decimals and negative values as well.

(c) $5(2x - 1) = 10$

Multiply brackets out first.

$10x - 5 = 10$

$10x = 10 + 5$

$10x = 15$

$x = \dfrac{10}{15} = 1.5.$

(d) $7x - 2 = 2x + 13$

Subtract $2x$ from both sides. Add two to both sides.

$7x - 2 - 2x = 13$

$5x = 13 + 2$

$5x = 15$

$x = \dfrac{15}{5} = 3.$

(e) $4(2n + 5) = 3(n + 10)$ Multiply brackets out first.

$8n + 20 = 3n + 30$

$8n + 20 - 3n = 30$

$5n = 30 - 20$

$5n = 10$

$n = \dfrac{10}{5} = 2.$

Using equations to solve problems

Example

Class 9A were playing a number game. Saima said "Multiplying my number by 5 and adding 8 gives the same answer as subtracting my number from 20."

(a) Call Saima's number y and form an equation.

$5y + 8 = 20 - y$

(b) Solve the equation to work out Saima's number:

$5y + 8 = 20 - y$

$5y + 8 + y = 20$

$6y = 20 - 8$

$6y = 12$

Check at the end that $y = 2$ works in the equation.

$y = \dfrac{12}{6} = 2.$ Saima's number is 2.

For
Level 7
only

Simultaneous equations

Two equations with two unknowns are called **simultaneous equations**.

They can be solved in several ways. Solving equations simultaneously involves finding values for the letters that will make both equations work.

Graphical method

The points at which any two graphs intersect represent the simultaneous solutions of these equations.

Example

Solve the simultaneous equations:
$y = 2x - 3$, $y - x = 1$ by a graphical method.

- Draw the two graphs:

  $y = 2x - 3$ If $x = 0$ $y = -3$.

  If $y = 0$ $x = \dfrac{3}{2}$.

  $y - x = 1$ If $x = 0$ $y = 1$.

  If $y = 0$ $x = -1$.

Work out the coordinates for when $x = 0$ and $y = 0$ to draw a quick graph.

- At the point of intersection $x = 4$ and $y = 5$.

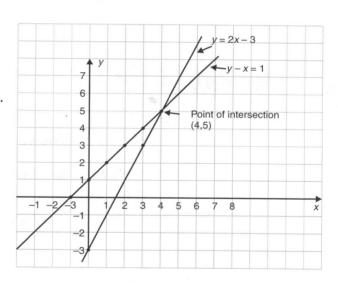

Elimination method

- If the coefficient of one of the letters is the same in both equations, then that letter may be eliminated by subtracting the equations.

The **coefficient** is the number a letter is multiplied by, e.g. the coefficient of $-3x$ is -3.

Example

Solve simultaneously $n + 3p = 25$, $2n + p = 15$.

$n + 3p = 25$ ①   Label the equations ① and ②.

$2n + p = 15$ ②   As no coefficients match, multiply equation ② by 3.

$6n + 3p = 45$ ③   The coefficients are now the same in equation ① and ③.

$5n + 0p = 20$ Subtract equation ① from equation ③.

So $5n = 20$,
i.e. $n = 4$.

$2n + p = 15$ Substitute the value of $n = 4$ into equation
so $8 + p = 15$,   ① or ②.
i.e. $p = 7$.

Always check that the values work.

Check in equation ① $4 + 3 \times 7 = 25$ ✓
(Substitute $n = 4$ and $p = 7$ into the other equation.)

The solution is $n = 4$ and $p = 7$.

To eliminate terms with **opposite** signs **add**.
To eliminate terms with **the same** signs **subtract**.

For Level 7 only

Inequalities

These are expressions where one side is **not equal** to the other. Inequalities are solved in a similar way to equations.

- Multiplying and dividing by negative numbers changes the direction of the sign. For example if $-x \geq 3$ then $x \leq -3$.

< is 'less than'
≤ is 'less than or equal to'
> is 'more than'
≥ is 'more than or equal to'

Examples

Solve the following inequality:

Use the same method that you used when solving equations.

$5x - 1 < 3x + 5$
$2x - 1 < 5$ Subtract 3x from both sides.
$2x < 6$ Add 1 to both sides.
$x < 3$ Divide both sides by 2.

The solution of the inequality may be represented on a number line.

Use ● when the end point is included and ○ when the end point is not included.

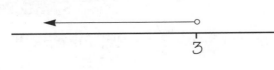

3

Equations and formulae
Questions

1 pattern 1   pattern 2   pattern 3

The diagram shows some patterns made up with sticks. If P represents the pattern number and S represents the number of sticks. Write down a formula connecting S and P.

2 Simplify these expressions:

(a) $5a + 2a + 3a$ (b) $6a - 2b + 5b$ (c) $3xy + 2yx$

(d) $5a \times 2b$ (e) $3a \times 4a$ (f) $6a + 2b - 2b + b$

3 A shape has the lengths as shown in the diagram. Write down an expression for the perimeter of the shape.

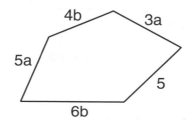

4 Some cards have the following expressions written on them:

A   B   C   D

$2a + 8$ $2a + 4$ $4a + 8$ $4a + 2$

Which card is the same as $4(a + 2)$?

5 Solve the following equations:

(a) $5a + 10 = 15$ (b) $\dfrac{n}{5} - 1 = 6$ (c) $5n + 1 = 11$

(d) $6n + 2 = 4n + 8$ (e) $6(n + 2) = 5n + 7$ (f) $2(n - 1) = 3(n + 4)$

For level 7 only
6 Solve these simultaneous equations:

$2x + 3y = 6$

$x + y = 1$

For level 7 only
7 Solve these inequalities:

(a) $3n + 2 < 6$ (b) $5n - 1 \le 2n + 5$

Shape, space and measure

Properties of shapes

Symmetry

Reflective symmetry

Examiner's tips and your notes

If asked to complete a shape to make it symmetrical use tracing paper to help.

- Both sides of a shape are symmetrical when a mirror line is drawn across it. The mirror line is known as the **line** or **axis of symmetry**.

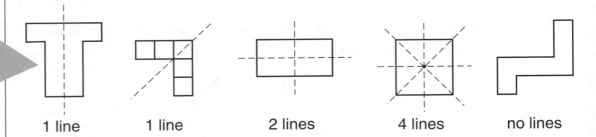

| 1 line | 1 line | 2 lines | 4 lines | no lines |

Rotational symmetry

- A 2D (two-dimensional) shape has rotational symmetry, if when it is turned, it looks exactly the same. The **order of rotational symmetry** is the number of times the shape turns and looks the same.

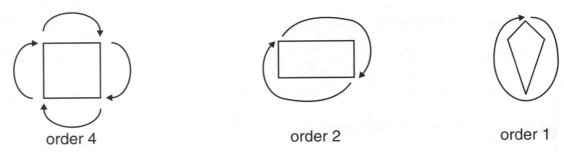

order 4   order 2   order 1

For the kite the shape has 1 position. It is said to have **rotational symmetry of order 1** or **no** rotational symmetry.

Plane symmetry

This is symmetry in 3D (three-dimensional) solids only.

A 3D shape has a plane of symmetry if the plane divides the shape into two halves, and one half is the exact mirror image of the other.

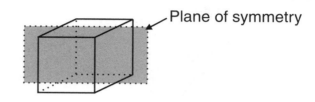

Plane of symmetry

2D shapes

Triangles

There are several types of triangles.

Right angled	Equilateral	Isosceles	Scalene

Has a 90° angle.	3 sides equal. 3 angles equal.	2 sides equal. Base angles equal.	No sides or angles the same.

Quadrilaterals

These are four-sided shapes.

Square	Rectangle
4 lines of symmetry. Rotational symmetry of order 4.	2 lines of symmetry. Rotational symmetry of order 2.

You need to be able to sketch these shapes and know their symmetrical properties.

Parallelogram

No lines of symmetry.
Rotational symmetry of order 2.

Rhombus

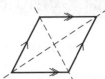

2 lines of symmetry.
Rotational symmetry of order 2.

Kite

No rotational symmetry.

1 line of symmetry.
No rotational symmetry.

Trapezium

Isosceles trapezium:
1 line of symmetry.
No rotational symmetry.

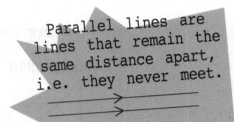

Parallel lines are lines that remain the same distance apart, i.e. they never meet.

Polygons

These are 2D shapes with **straight** sides. **Regular polygons** are shapes with all sides and angles equal.

Number of sides	Name of polygon
3	Triangle
4	Quadrilateral
5	Pentagon
6	Hexagon
7	Heptagon
8	Octagon

3D shapes

Cube	Cuboid	Sphere	Cylinder	Cone
	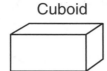			

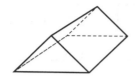

Triangular prism

Square-based pyramid

Drawing shapes

Nets of solids

The net of a 3D shape is a 2D shape which is folded to make the 3D shape.

When making the shape remember to put tabs on to stick together.

Examples

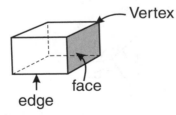

Vertex

face

edge

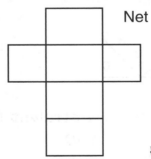

Net

When asked to draw an accurate net, you must measure carefully.

Triangular prism

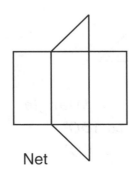

Net

Plans and elevations

A **plan** is what is seen if a 3D shape is looked down on from above.

An **elevation** is seen if the 3D shape is looked at from the side or front.

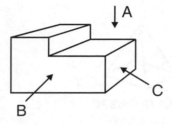

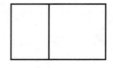

Plan
A.

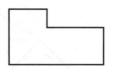

Front elevation
B.

Side elevation
C.

Angles

An **acute** angle is between 0° and 90°.

An **obtuse** angle is between 90° and 180°.

A **reflex** angle is between 180° and 360°.

A **right angle** is 90°.

Angle facts

You must remember these angle facts as you will need to apply them to questions.

Angles on a **straight line** add up to **180°**
$a + b + c = 180°$.

Angles at a **point** add up to **360°**
$a + b + c = 360°$.

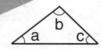

Angles in a **triangle** add up to **180°**
$a + b + c = 180°$.

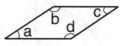

Angles in a **quadrilateral** add up to **360°**
$a + b + c + d = 360°$.

Vertically opposite angles
a = b, c = d.
a + c = b + d = 180°.

An **exterior angle** of a triangle equals the sum of the two opposite **interior angles**.
a + b = c.

Angles in parallel lines

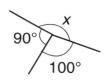

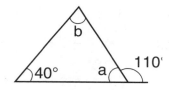

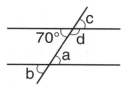

Alternate (z) angles are **equal**.

Corresponding angles are **equal**.

Supplementary angles add up to **180°**
c + d = 180°.

Examples

Find the angles labelled by letters:

x + 90° + 100°
  = 360°
x = 360° − 190°
x = 170°.

a + 110° = 180°
a = 70°.
70° + 40° + b
  = 180°
b = 180° − 110°
b = 70°.

a = 70° (alternate).
b = 70° (corresponding).
c = 70° (corresponding
        to a).
d = 180 − 70 = 110°
    (angles on a straight
    line).

Show full working out.

Reading angles

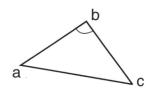

When asked to find abc or ∠abc or ab̂c, find the angle shown by the **middle letter**, in this case b.

Angles in polygons

There are two types of angles in a polygon: **interior** (inside) and **exterior** (outside).

For a polygon with n sides:

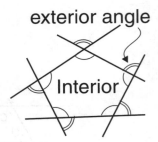

- Sum of exterior angles = 360°.

  So exterior angle = $\dfrac{360°}{n}$.

- Interior angle + exterior angle = 180°.

- Sum of interior angles = $(n - 2) \times 180°$.

Example

Calculate the interior and exterior angle of a regular pentagon.

A pentagon has 5 sides, i.e. $n = 5$.

Exterior angle = $\dfrac{360}{5}$ = 72°.

Interior angle + exterior angle = 180°.

Interior angle = 180° − 72°
                = 108°.

For
level 7
only

Pythagoras' theorem

The **hypotenuse** is the longest side of a right-angled triangle. It is always opposite the right angle.

Pythagoras' theorem states: in any right-angled triangle, the square on the hypotenuse is equal to the sum of the squares on the other two sides.

Pythagoras' theorem allows you to calculate the length of a side providing the lengths of the other two sides are known.

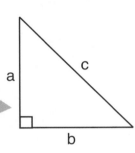

Using the letters in the diagram the theorem is written as:

$$c^2 = a^2 + b^2$$

This may be rearranged to give:

$$b^2 = c^2 - a^2 \cdot$$

$$a^2 = c^2 - b^2$$

These are useful when calculating shorter sides.

Example

Find the length of XY, giving your answer to 1 d.p. Using Pythagoras' theorem gives:

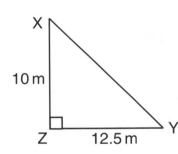

$$XY^2 = XZ^2 + ZY^2$$
$$= 10^2 + 12.5^2$$

$$XY^2 = 256.25$$

$$XY^2 = \sqrt{256.25} \quad \text{Square root to find XY.}$$
$$= 16.0 \text{ m (1 d.p.).}$$

Example

Find the length of CD, giving your answer to 1 d.p. Using Pythagoras' theorem gives:

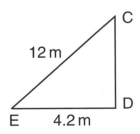

$$CE^2 = CD^2 + DE^2$$

$$CD^2 = CE^2 - DE^2$$

Rearrange the formula and use $a^2 = c^2 - b^2$.

$$CD^2 = 12^2 - 4.2^2$$

$$CD^2 = 126.36$$

$$CD = \sqrt{126.36}$$

11.2 m (1 d.p.).

Properties of shapes
Questions

1 The dotted lines are the lines of symmetry. Complete the shape so that it is symmetrical.

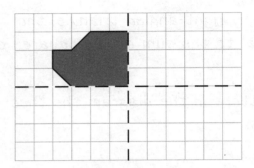

2 What is the name of a six-sided polygon?

3 Draw an accurate net of this 3D shape.

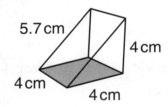

4 Find the size of the angles labelled by letters:

(a)

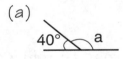

(b)

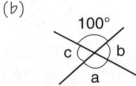

(c)

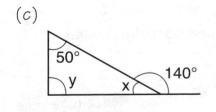

(d)

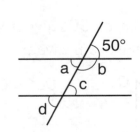

5 Find the size of (a) an exterior (b) an interior angle of a regular hexagon.

6 Calculate the lengths of the sides marked with a letter. Give your answer to 1 d.p.

(a)

(b)

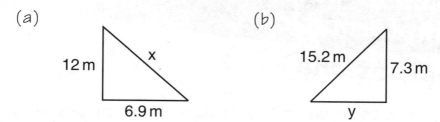

7 A ship sets off from Port A and travels 50 km North then 80 km East to reach Port B. How far is Port A from Port B, by the shortest route?

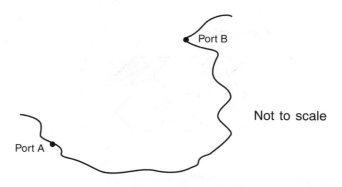

Not to scale

Properties of position, movement and transformation

Tessellations

- A tessellation is a pattern of 2D shapes which fit together without leaving any gaps.

- For shapes to tessellate, the angles at each point must add up to 360°.

Example

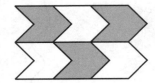

Bearings

- Bearings give a direction in degrees.

- Bearings are always measured from the **North** in a **clockwise** direction. They must have **3 figures**.

Examples

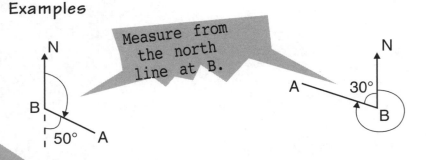

The word 'from' is very important. It tells you where to put the north line and measure from.

Bearing of A **from** B
= 180° − 50° = 130°.

Bearing of A **from** B
= 360° − 30° = 330°.

When finding the **back bearing** (the bearing of B **from** A above)

- draw a North line at A

- use the properties of parallel lines, since both North lines are parallel.

Examples

Look for
alternate (Z)
or
corresponding
angles.

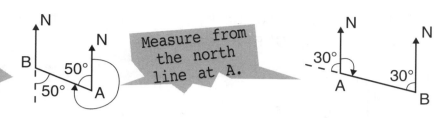

Measure from
the north
line at A.

Bearing of B from A
= 360° − 50°
= 310°.

Bearing of B from A
= 180° − 30°
= 150°.

Transformations

• A **transformation** changes the **position** or **size** of a shape.

Rotations

• Rotations turn a figure through an angle about some fixed point. This fixed point is called the **centre of rotation**.

• The size or shape of the figure is not changed.

Notice that
the rotated
shapes are
congruent,
that is they
are exactly
the same
size and
shape.

Example

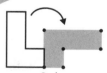

0 (centre of rotation)

This is a 90° rotation about O, in a clockwise direction (also known as a $\frac{1}{4}$ turn clockwise).

Enlargements

• These change the size but not the shape of an object.

• The **centre of enlargement** is the point from which the enlargement takes place.

• The **scale factor** indicates how many times the length of the original figure has changed size.

• If the scale factor is **greater than 1**, the shape becomes **bigger**.

• If the scale factor is **less than 1**, the shape becomes **smaller**.

For
Level 7
only

Example

Enlarge shape ABCDEF by a scale factor of 2, centre = (O, O).
Call it A′ B′ C′ D′ E′ F′.

If asked to describe an enlargement, state the centre of enlargement and the scale factor.

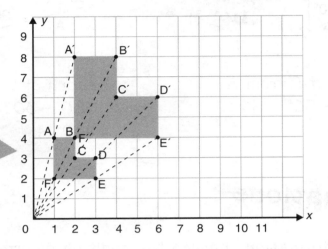

Notice that each side of the enlargement is twice the size of the original.

OA′ = 2OA.

Example

For Level 7 only

ABC has been enlarged with a scale factor = $\frac{1}{2}$, to give A′B′C′ centre of enlargement at O.

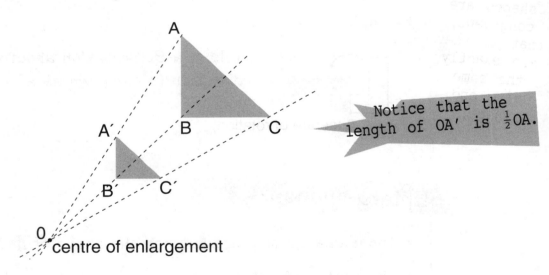

Notice that the length of OA′ is $\frac{1}{2}$OA.

LOGO

- This is a computer program which is used to draw shapes.

- Transformations can take place using LOGO.

Example

Shape Y is an equilateral triangle. The instructions to draw shape Y are:

FORWARD 4.

TURN RIGHT 120°.

FORWARD 4.

TURN RIGHT 120°.

FORWARD 4.

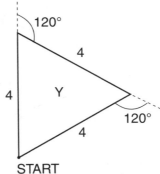

Constructions

The perpendicular bisector of a line

- Draw a line XY.

- Draw two arcs, with the compasses using X as the centre. The compasses must be set at a radius greater than half the distance of XY.

- Draw two more arcs with Y as the centre (keep the compasses the same distance apart as before).

- Join the two points where the arcs cross.

- AB is the **perpendicular bisector** of XY.

- N is the **midpoint** of XY.

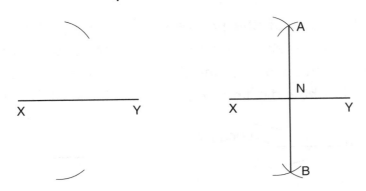

Bisecting an angle

- Draw two lines XY and YZ to meet at an angle.
- Using compasses, place the point at Y and draw the two arcs on XY and YZ.
- Place the compass points at the two arcs on XY and YZ and draw arcs to cross at N. Join Y to N.

YN is the **bisector** of angle XYZ.

Practise by bisecting your own angles.

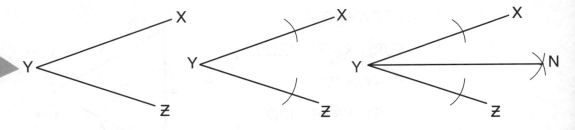

For Level 7 only

Locus

- The locus of a point is the set of all possible positions which that point can occupy, subject to some given condition or rule.
- The plural of locus is **loci**.

Common loci

(a) The locus of the points which are a constant distance from a fixed point is a circle.

(b) The locus of the points which are equidistant from two points XY is the perpendicular bisector of XY.

Locus must be drawn carefully and measured accurately.

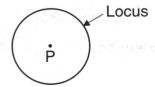

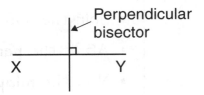

(c) The locus of the points which are equidistant from two lines is the line which bisects the angle.

(d) The locus of the points which are a constant distance from a line XY is a pair of parallel lines, above and below XY.

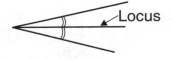

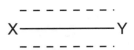

Example

John is redesigning his garden. He wishes to plant a rose tree. The tree must be at least 4 m from the house, and at least 4 m from the corner A of the greenhouse. Using a scale of 1 cm to 2 m, show accurately on the diagram the region in which John can plant his rose tree.

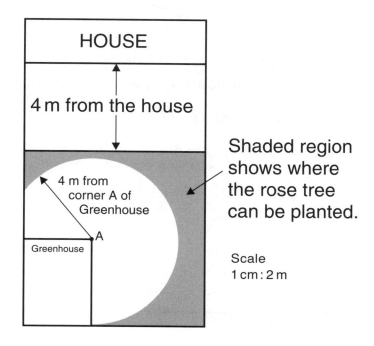

HOUSE

4 m from the house

4 m from corner A of Greenhouse

A

Greenhouse

Shaded region shows where the rose tree can be planted.

Scale
1 cm : 2 m

Properties of position, movement and transformation
Questions

1 What are the bearings of X from Y in the following:

(a)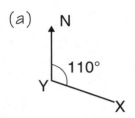

(b)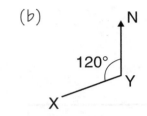

(c)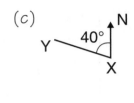

2 Enlarge shape P by (a) a scale factor of 2, call it A.

(b) a scale factor of $\frac{1}{2}$, call it B.

Centre of enlargement is at (0, 0).

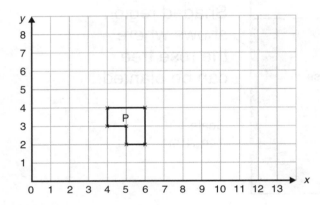

3 Shape A is a rectangle.

Complete the LOGO commands for drawing the rectangle:

FORWARD 2.

TURN RIGHT 90°.

FORWARD 5.

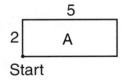

4 Bisect this angle:

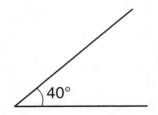

For
level 7
only ▶

5 A gold coin is buried in the rectangular field. It is

(a) 4 m from T

(b) Equidistant
    from RU
    and RS.

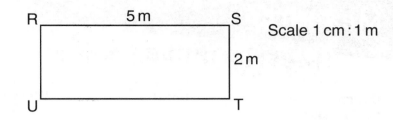

Mark with an X the position of the gold coin.

Measures

Metric units

Length	Weight	Capacity
10 mm = 1 cm	1000 mg = 1 g	1000 ml = 1 l
100 cm = 1 m	1000 g = 1 kg	100 cl = 1 l
1000 m = 1 km	1000 kg = 1 tonne	1000 cm^3 = 1 l

Converting units

- If changing from **small** units to **large** units (e.g. g to kg) **divide**.
- If changing from **large** units to **small** units (e.g. km to m) **multiply**.

Examples

500 cm = 5 m (÷ 100).　　　5 l = 500 cl (× 100).

3500 g = 3.5 kg (÷ 1000).　25 cm = 250 mm (× 10).

Imperial units

Length	Weight	Capacity
1 foot = 12 inches	1 stone = 14 pounds (lb)	20 fluid oz = 1 pint
1 yard = 3 feet	1 pound = 16 ounces (oz)	8 pints = 1 gallon

Comparisons between metric and imperial units

Length	Weight	Capacity
2.5 cm ≈ 1 inch	25 g ≈ 1 ounce	1 litre ≈ $1\frac{3}{4}$ pints
30 cm ≈ 1 foot	1 kg ≈ 2.2 pounds	4.5 litres ≈ 1 gallon
1 m ≈ 39 inches		
8 km ≈ 5 miles		

Example

Change 8 inches into cm.

1 inch ≈ 2.5 cm.

8 inches = 8 × 2.5 = 20 cm.

> Check to see if your answer sounds sensible.

For Level 7 only

Accuracy of measurement

Continuous measurements

- These are measurements which have been made by using a measuring instrument; for example the height of a person.

- Continuous measures are **not exact**.

Example

Lucy is 167 cm tall correct to the nearest cm. Her actual height could be anywhere between 166.5 cm and 167.5 cm.

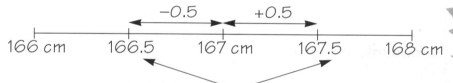

These two values are the limits of Lucy's height.
If H represents height, then

$$166.5 \leq H < 167.5$$

This is the **lower limit** of Lucy's height. Anything below 166.5 is recorded as 166 cm.

This is the **upper limit** of Lucy's height. Anything from 167.5 upwards would be recorded as 168 cm.

Remember that these measurements cannot be equal to the upper limit.

In general, if a measurement is accurate to some given amount, then the true value lies within a maximum of a half a unit of that amount.

Areas and volumes

Perimeter – this is the distance around the outside edge of a shape.

Area – this is the amount of space a 2D shape covers. Common units of area are mm², cm², m², etc.

Volume – this is the amount of space a 3D shape occupies. Common units of volume are mm³, cm³, m³, etc.

Areas of quadrilaterals and triangles

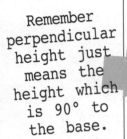

Remember perpendicular height just means the height which is 90° to the base.

Area of a rectangle

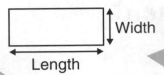

Write the formulae using letters. It's quicker.

Area = Length × Width.

$A = L \times W.$

Area of a parallelogram

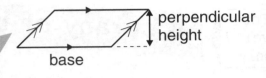

perpendicular height

base

Area = Base × Perpendicular height.

$A = b \times h.$

Area of a triangle

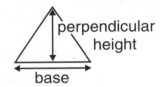

perpendicular height

base

$A = \frac{1}{2} \times$ Base × Perpendicular height.

$A = \frac{1}{2} \times b \times h.$

Area of a trapezium

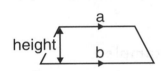

height

a

b

$A = \frac{1}{2} \times$ (Sum of parallel sides) × Perpendicular height.

$A = \frac{1}{2} \times (a + b) \times h.$

Examples

Find the area of the following shapes.

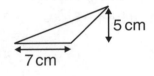

5 cm

7 cm

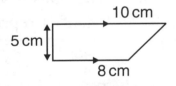

10 cm

5 cm

8 cm

$A = \frac{1}{2} \times b \times h.$

$A = \frac{1}{2} \times 7 \times 5 = 17.5 \ cm^2.$

$A = \frac{1}{2} \times (a + b) \times h.$

$A = \frac{1}{2} \times (10 + 8) \times 5 = 45 \ cm^2.$

Circumference and area of a circle

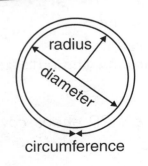

radius

diameter

circumference

Circumference $= \pi \times$ diameter $C = \pi \times d$

$= 2 \times \pi \times$ radius $= 2 \times \pi \times r$

Area $= \pi \times (radius)^2$ $A = \pi \times r^2$

Remember r^2 means $r \times r.$

Remember that the circumference of a circle is the distance around the outside edge.

Example

Mohammed's bicycle wheel has a diameter of 60 cm. Work out the circumference of the wheel, using $\pi = 3.14$.

$C = \pi \times d$

$C = 3.14 \times 60$

$C = 188.4$ cm

Use $\pi = 3.14$ or the value of π on your calculator, if you are not told in the question.

If Mohammed travels a distance of 50 m on the bicycle, how many times does his wheel turn around?

Change 50 m into cm first, i.e. $50 \times 100 = 5000$ cm

Distance ÷ Circumference = No. of turns.

$\dfrac{5000}{188.4} = 26.5$ times.

Check that the answer is sensible.

Always check the units are the same before starting a question.

The wheel must turn 27 times to go a distance of 50 m.

Example

Find the area of a circular rose garden, which has a diameter of 2.6 m. Use $\pi = 3.142$.

Diameter = 2.6 m

Radius = $2.6 \div 2 = 1.3$ m.

Area = $\pi \times r^2$
     = 3.142×1.3^2.   Remember 1.3^2 means 1.3×1.3.
     = 5.3 m² (1 d.p.).

Volumes of 3D shapes

Volume of a cuboid

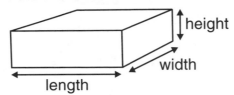

Volume =
Length × Width × Height

$V = l \times w \times h.$

Volume of a prism

Volume =
Area of cross-section × Length

$V = a \times l.$

A prism is any solid which can be cut into slices, which are all the same shape. This is called having a **uniform cross-section**.

67

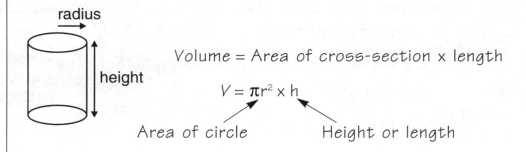

For
Level 7
only

Volume of a cylinder

radius

height

Volume = Area of cross-section x length

$$V = \pi r^2 \times h$$

Area of circle   Height or length

Example

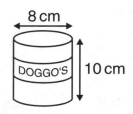

8 cm

DOGGO'S 10 cm

Dog food is sold in a cylindrical tin.
Work out the volume of dog food the tin contains.
Use $\pi = 3.14$.

$$V = \pi \times r^2 \times h$$

$$V = 3.14 \times 4^2 \times 10$$

$$V = 502.4 \ cm^2.$$

Diameter = 8 cm,
i.e. Radius = 4 cm.

Example

A door wedge is in the shape of a trapezium.
Work out the volume of the door wedge.

Area of cross-section:

$$A = \frac{(a + b) \times h}{2}$$

$$\frac{(3 + 8) \times 5}{2} = 27.5 \ cm^2$$

Volume = $27.5 \times 4 = 110 \ cm^3$.

Substitute
values in
carefully
and show
full working
out.

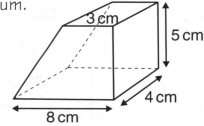

3 cm   5 cm

4 cm

8 cm

Remember to find the
volume, multiply the area
of cross-section by the
length.

Measures
Questions

or
vel
7
ıly

1 Change 6200 g into kg.

2 Change 4.2 cm into mm.

3 Change 6 litres into pints.

4 Write down the upper and lower limits for a time of 6.3 seconds, rounded to the nearest tenth of a second.

5 Work out the area of the following shapes, giving your answer to 1 d.p.

(a)
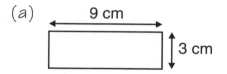

(b)
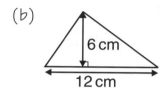

(c)
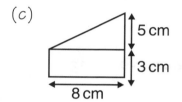

(d)
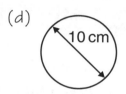

6 Work out the volume of these 3D shapes, giving your answer to 1 d.p.

(a)
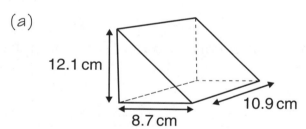

For Level 7 only

(b) 10.6 cm
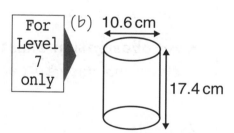

7 Work out the circumference of a circle with radius of 4.9 cm. Use π = 3.14.

Handling data

Processing and interpreting data

Types of data

Examiner's tips and your notes

- **Discrete data** – each category is separate. It is often found by counting. Examples include the number of red cars in a car park.

- **Continuous data** – here the values change from one category to the next. Such data is often found by measuring. Examples include the height and shoe size of year 8 pupils.

Surveys and questionnaires

- Data can be collected by carrying out **surveys** using **questionnaires**.

- A **hypothesis** is a prediction which can be tested and usually gives a purpose to the survey, i.e. most staff at the school have a red car.

- An **observation sheet** is used to collect data. They must be clear and easy to use.

Example

Colour of staff cars		
Colour	Tally	Frequency
red		
blue		
white		
green		
black		
others		

Questionnaires

When designing questionnaires:

- Keep the questionnaire short.

- Give instructions on how to fill it in.

Word any questions you write very carefully.

- Ask questions which cover the purpose of your survey.

- Do not ask for information which is not needed, e.g. name.

- Make sure that your opinion is not evident, e.g. do you agree that 'Neighbours' is better than 'Home and Away'?

- Allow for any possible outcomes:

Example

How much do you spend on magazines each week?

Under £1 ☐   £1–£2 ☐   £2.01–£3 ☐   over £3 ☐

Collecting information

- Data which has been collected can be sorted by putting it into a table called a **tally chart** or **frequency table**.

- The tally chart shows the frequency of each item (how often the item occurs).

- A tally is just a line of I, which are grouped into fives to make them easier to count. The fifth one forms a gate, i.e. ⃥⃥⃥⃥.

Grouping data

If the data covers a large range of results, it is usual to group the data into **class intervals**, where each class interval is the same width. For continuous data the class intervals are often written using **inequalities**.

Example

The heights in cm of 30 pupils were:

To help: cross off the data as you put it in the table.

137	142	139	120	152
126	149	147	138	135
135	132	127	154	150
138	144	149	150	122
140	142	138	141	149
127	125	141	140	135

Height (cm)	Tally	Frequency
120 ≤ h <125	II	2
125 ≤ h <130	IIII	4
130 ≤ h <135	I	1
135 ≤ h <140	IIII III	8
140 ≤ h <145	HHI II	7
145 ≤ h <150	IIII	4
150 ≤ h <155	IIII	4
	Total	30

Always check the total at the end to make sure all data is included.

- The data has been grouped into class intervals of 5.

- Choose sensible groupings of 2, 5, or 10.

- Check that all data has been included.

$120 ≤ h < 125$ means that the heights are all between 120 and 125 cm.

$120 ≤ h$ means that the height can be equal to 120 cm.

$h < 125$ means that the height cannot be equal to 125 cm. It would be in the next group.

Representing information

Pie charts

- These are circles split up into sections. Each section represents a certain number of items.

Calculating angles for a pie chart

- Find the total for the items listed.

- Find the fraction of the total for each item.

- Multiply the fraction by 360° to find the angle.

Remember there are 360° at the centre of the circle.

Example

The favourite sports of 24 students in year 9.

Sport	Frequency
Football	9
Swimming	5
Netball	3
Hockey	7

Finding the angle

9 out of 24 like football, i.e. $\dfrac{9}{24} \times 360° = 135°$.

fraction ← 24

multiply by 360°.

Key in on the calculator:

9 ÷ 24 × 360 =

$\text{Football} = \frac{9}{24} \times 360° = 135°$

$\text{Swimming} = \frac{5}{24} \times 360° = 75°$

$\text{Netball} = \frac{3}{24} \times 360° = 45°$

$\text{Hockey} = \frac{7}{24} \times 360° = 105°$

$\text{Total} = 360°$

Check that your angles add up to 360°

Measure the angles carefully with a protractor.

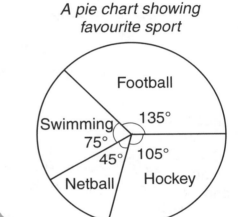

A pie chart showing favourite sport

Interpreting pie charts

The pie chart shows how some students travel to school.

There are 18 students in total.

How many travel by (a) Car?

(b) Bus?

(c) Walk?

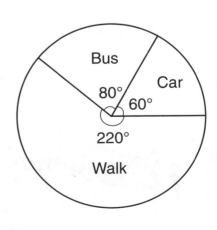

$360° = 18 \text{ students}$

$1° = \dfrac{18}{360°} = 0.05 \text{ (work out 1°)}$

Car = $60° \times 0.05 = 3$ students.

Bus = $80° \times 0.05 = 4$ students.

Walk = $220° \times 0.05 = 11$ students.

Frequency diagrams

- These are drawn to illustrate **continuous data**.

- They are similar to bar charts except there are no gaps between the bars.

- The data must be grouped into equal class intervals if the length of the bar is used to represent the frequency.

Example

The heights of 30 pupils are grouped as shown in the table.

- The axes do not need to start at zero.

- Do not leave a gap between the bars.

- Label the axes and write a title.

Height (cm)	Frequency
$120 \leq h < 125$	2
$125 \leq h < 130$	4
$130 \leq h < 135$	1
$135 \leq h < 140$	8
$140 \leq h < 145$	7
$145 \leq h < 150$	4
$150 \leq h < 155$	4
	30

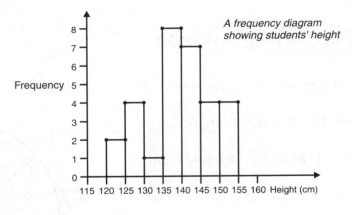

A frequency diagram showing students' height

Frequency polygons

- These are used to join the midpoints of the class intervals for grouped or continuous data.

- To draw the frequency polygon put a cross on the middle of the bar and join the crosses up with a ruler.

- Draw a line down from the middle of the first and last bar to the x axis.

Example

Consider the frequency diagram of the students' height.

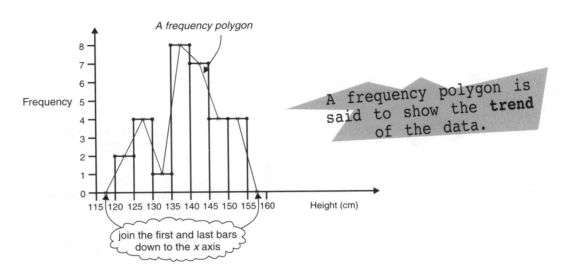

A frequency polygon is said to show the **trend** of the data.

join the first and last bars down to the *x* axis

Scatter diagrams

- A scatter diagram (scattergraph) is used to show two sets of data at the same time.

- It is used to show the connection (**correlation**) between two sets of data. There are three types of correlation: **positive**, **negative** or **zero**.

In the SATs examination, you must be able to describe types of correlation.

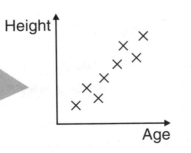

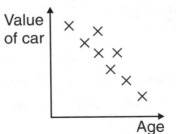

Positive correlation – this is when as one value increases so does the other.

Negative correlation – this is when as one value increases the other decreases.

Zero correlation – this is when there is no connection between the values.

75

Drawing scatter diagrams

- Work out the scales first before starting. Plot the points carefully, ticking off each point in the table as it is plotted.

Example

The data shows the age of several cars and how much they are now worth.

AGE (years)	1	8	4	7	6	3	5	7	3	5	2
PRICE (£)	5200	1200	3400	1800	2800	4000	1800	2400	4400	3000	5000

> Plot the points carefully since it is easy to make mistakes.

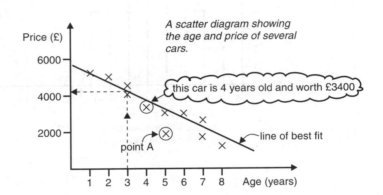

A scatter diagram showing the age and price of several cars.

this car is 4 years old and worth £3400

- The scatter diagram shows that the older the cars become the less they are worth, i.e. there is a **negative correlation**.

- **Point A** shows a car which is 5 years old and worth £1800. This is slightly less than expected and may be due to rust or a dent, etc.

> You need to be able to interpret the scatter diagram.

> For Level 7 only

Line of best fit

- This is the line which 'best fits' the data. It goes in the direction of the data and has roughly the same number of points above the line as below it.

- A line of 'best fit' can be used to make predictions.

Example

Sandra wishes to sell her car. If it is 3 years old roughly how much would she expect to receive?

- Go across to 3 years on the horizontal axis. Read up to the line of best fit and then read across. Approximately £4100.

Misleading graphs

- Statistical graphs are sometimes misleading, they do not tell the true story.

Examples

In the exam make any criticisms clear.

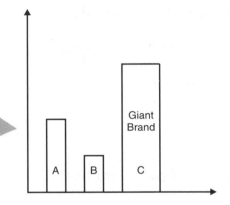

This graph is misleading because it has no scales and the bars are not the same width.

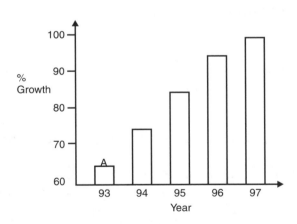

This graph is misleading because the scales do not start at zero, so the growth looks much bigger than it actually is.

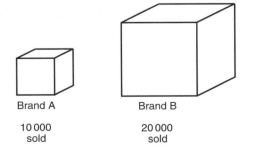

This pictogram is misleading because the pictures change size. Although Brand B has only sold twice the amount of Brand A it gives the impression of having sold much more.

Averages

There are three types of averages: **mean**, **median** and the **mode**.

Mean – sometimes known as the 'average'

$$\text{Mean} = \frac{\text{total number of items}}{\text{number of items used}}.$$

Median – the middle value when the numbers are put in order of size.

Mode – the one that occurs the most often.

Range – this tells us how much the information is spread.

Range = highest value – lowest value.

Example

A football team scored the following number of goals in their first ten matches:

2, 4, 0, 1, 2, 2, 3, 6, 2, 4.

Find the mean, median, mode and range of the number of goals scored.

$$\text{Mean} = \frac{2+4+0+1+2+2+3+6+2+4}{10} = \frac{26}{10} = 2.6 \text{ goals.}$$

Do not round off.

Median = 0, 1, 2, 2, 2, 2, 3, 4, 4, 6   Put in order of size first.

0̸ 1̸ 2̸ 2̸ ⟨2 2⟩ 3̸ 4̸ 4̸ 6̸   Cross off from the ends to find the middle.

$$\frac{2+2}{2} = 2 \text{ goals.}$$

If there are two numbers in the middle the median is halfway between them.

Mode = 2 goals, because it occurs 4 times.

Range = 6 – 0 = 6.

Remember to subtract the two values in order to obtain the range.

Finding averages from a frequency table

- A frequency table tells us **how many** are in a group.

Example

Charlotte made this frequency table for the number of minutes late students were to registration:

Number of minutes late (x)	0	1	2	3	4
Frequency (f)	10	4	6	3	2

This tells us that 4 students were 1 minute late for registration.

Two students were four minutes late.

Mean = Total of the results when multiplied

Total of the frequency

$$= \frac{(10 \times 0) + (4 \times 1) + (6 \times 2) + (3 \times 3) + (2 \times 4)}{(10 + 4 + 6 + 3 + 2)}$$

$$= \frac{0 + 4 + 12 + 9 + 8}{25} = \frac{33}{25} = 1.32 \text{ minutes late.}$$

Remember to add up the total frequency.

Median

There are 25 students in the class, the middle person is the 13th.

From the frequency table:

Number of minutes late (x)	0	1	2	3	4
Frequency (f)	10	4	6	3	2

the first 10 students

the 13th student is in here.

Median number of minutes late is 1.

Mode

This is the one that has the highest frequency.

Mode = 0 minutes late because it had a
frequency higher than any others.

Range = $4 - 0 = 4$ minutes.

> Remember to write down the answer zero, not the number 10 (this is the frequency).

For Level 7 only

Averages of grouped data

Mean

- When the data is grouped, the exact data is not known.
- Estimate by using the **midpoint** of the **class interval**.
- The midpoint is the halfway value.

Example

The weight of year 9 pupils.

Weight (kg)	Frequency (f)	Midpoint (x)	fx
$40 \leq W < 45$	7	42.5	297.5
$45 \leq W < 50$	4	47.5	190
$50 \leq W < 55$	3	52.5	157.5
$55 \leq W < 60$	1	57.5	57.5

- This is the same as before except the frequency is multiplied by the midpoint.

$$\text{Mean} = \frac{\sum fx}{\sum f} = \frac{(7 \times 42.5) + (4 \times 47.5) + (3 \times 52.5) + (1 \times 57.5)}{7 + 4 + 3 + 1}$$

$$= \frac{702.5}{15} = 46.8 \text{ kg (1 d.p.)}$$

Mode When using grouped data only the modal class can be found. This is the class with the highest frequency.

Modal class = $40 \leq W < 45$

Comparing sets of data

- The range and averages are used to compare sets of data.

Example

9A obtained a mean of 57% in a test.

9T obtained a mean of 84% in the same test.

From the averages we would say 9T is better than 9A. However if we look at the range:

9A = 100% − 21% = 79%.

9T = 94% − 76% = 18%.

Using the range it can be seen that not all of 9T are better than 9A, because some of 9A obtained higher marks than 9T. The average for 9A has been lowered because of the low marks obtained by some pupils.

Use the range when comparing data.

Processing and interpreting data
Questions

1 A chocolate firm asked 1440 students which type of chocolate they preferred. The pie chart shows the results. How many people preferred:

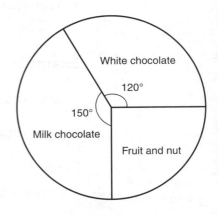

(a) White chocolate?

(b Fruit and nut?

(c) Milk chocolate?

2 Look at the two graphs below.

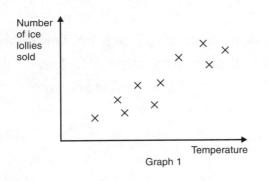

Graph 1

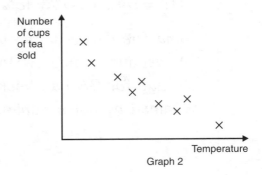

Graph 2

(a) What does graph 1 tell you about the relationship between the number of ice lollies sold and the temperature?

(b) What does graph 2 tell you about the relationship between the number of cups of tea sold and the temperature?

3 Using the histogram opposite, complete the frequency table below.

(a)

Thumb length	Frequency
$2 \leq L < 4$	
$4 \leq L < 6$	
$6 \leq L < 8$	7
$8 \leq L < 10$	
$10 \leq L < 12$	

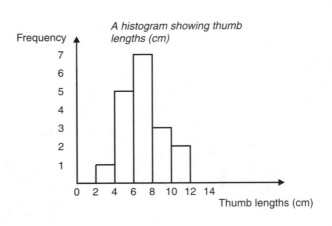

A histogram showing thumb lengths (cm)

(b) How many people were in the survey?

(c) Draw a frequency polygon on the histogram.

4 Find the mean, median, mode and range of this data:

2, 4, 1, 1, 2, 3, 7, 5, 5, 5, 2, 5, 6.

5 The length of the roots of some plants are recorded in the table below.

Length (cm)	Frequency (f)	Midpoint (x)
$0 \leq L < 5$	7	
$5 \leq L < 10$	9	
$10 \leq L < 15$	4	
$15 \leq L < 20$	2	

(a) Find an estimate for the mean length.

(b) What is the modal class?

6 This question was included in a survey. 'Do you agree that swimming lessons should only take place on a Saturday morning?' What is wrong with the question?

Estimating and calculating the possibilities of events

Probability

- This is the chance that something will happen.

- Probabilities must be written as either a **fraction**, **decimal** or **percentage**. **Never** write the words 'Out of'.

- Probabilities can be shown on a probability scale. All probabilities lie between 0 and 1. No event has a probability greater than 1.

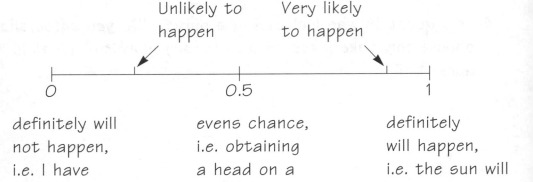

Exhaustive events account for all possible outcomes, i.e. the list 1, 2, 3, 4, 5, 6 gives all possible outcomes when a fair die is thrown.

Probability in practice

- Estimates of probability can be carried out by experiment, surveys or symmetrical properties of the shape.

Example

It could be said that the next car to pass the school is blue only after a survey has been conducted.

Calculating probabilities

- Probabilities can be calculated using the fact that each outcome is equally likely.

Probability of an event = Number of ways an event can happen
                              Total number of outcomes

P (event) is the shortened way of writing the probability of an event.

Example

There are 12 socks in a drawer, 3 are red, 4 are blue and the rest are black. Nigel picks out a sock at random. What is the probability that the sock he has pulled out is:

(a) blue?   (b) red?   (c) black?   (d) blue, red or black?
(e) green?

Make sure that the number on the bottom is the total number of outcomes.

(a) $p(\text{blue}) = \frac{4}{12} = \frac{1}{3}$

(b) $p(\text{red}) = \frac{3}{12} = \frac{1}{4}$

(c) $p(\text{black}) = \frac{5}{12}$

(d) $p(\text{blue, red or black}) = \frac{12}{12} = 1$

(e) $p(\text{green}) = \frac{0}{12}$

All probabilities add up to 1, i.e. choosing a blue, red or black will definitely happen.

There are no green socks in the drawer so the event will definitely not happen.

Probability of an event not happening

If two events cannot happen at the same time:

p(event will not happen) = 1 − p(event will happen)

To find the probability that an event will not happen:

• Find the probability the event will happen.

• Subtract it from 1.

Example

The probability that it rains today is $\frac{7}{11}$. What is the probability that it will not rain?

Use the fraction key on your calculator to help.

$p(\text{not rain}) = 1 - p(\text{will rain})$

$p(\text{not rain}) = 1 - \frac{7}{11} = \frac{4}{11}.$

Example

The probability that the torch works is 0.53. What is the probability that it does not work?

To quickly check add both numbers up and make sure you get 1.

$p(\text{does not work}) = 1 - p(\text{works})$

$p(\text{does not work}) = 1 - 0.53 = 0.47.$

Expected number

• Probability can be used to estimate the expected number of times an event is likely to occur.

Example

If a die is thrown 180 times, approximately how many twos am I likely to obtain?

Remember there are 6 outcomes on a die.

$p(2) = \frac{1}{6} \times 180 = 30$ two's.

Since a 2 is expected $\frac{1}{6}$ of the time.

Key in on the calculator: 1 ÷ 6 × 180 =

Example

The probability that Ellie obtains full marks on a spelling test is 0.4. If she takes 30 spelling tests in a year, in how many tests would you expect her to make no mistakes?

$0.4 \times 30 = 12$ tests.

For Level 7 only

Relative frequencies

• If a die is thrown 180 times, we have shown that approximately 30 twos would be obtained. When experiments like this are used to estimate probabilities it is known as the **relative frequency** that the event will happen.

Relative frequency of an event =

Relative frequency is used as an estimate of probability.

$$\frac{\textbf{Number of times the event occurred}}{\textbf{Total number of trials}}$$

• As the number of throws increases the relative frequency will get closer to the expected probability.

Example

When a fair coin was thrown 80 times, a Head came up 35 times. What is the relative frequency of getting a Head?

Number of trials = 80.   Relative frequency = $\frac{35}{80}$ = 0.4375.

Number of heads = 35.

The **theoretical** probability = $\frac{1}{2}$ = 0.5.

Possible outcomes for two events

- Using lists, diagrams and tables are helpful when there are outcomes of two events.

- These tables are sometimes known as sample space diagrams.

Examples

For his lunch Matthew can choose a main course and a pudding.

List all the possible outcomes of his lunch.

Menu	
Main Courses	**Puddings**
Pizza	Apple Pie
Chicken	Lemon Tart
Salad	

Try and write out the outcomes in a well ordered way.

Pizza, Apple pie   Chicken, Apple pie   Salad, Apple pie

Pizza, Lemon tart   Chicken, Lemon tart   Salad, Lemon tart

There are 6 possible outcomes.

Example

The spinner and the die are thrown together, and their scores are added.

Represent the outcomes on a sample space diagram.

It may help to put a ring or square around the numbers you need.

- There are 18 outcomes.

   (a) The p(score of 6) = $\frac{3}{18}$ = $\frac{1}{6}$.

   (b) The p(multiple of 4) = $\frac{5}{18}$.

2 on the spinner, 6 on the die, 2 + 6 = 8

Spinner

2	3	④	5	⑥	7	⑧
2	3	④	5	⑥	7	⑧
1	2	3	④	5	⑥	7

1	2	3	4	5	6

Die

Estimating and calculating the possibilities of events

Questions

1 On the number line below place the arrows on the scale to show these probabilities:

(a) I will obtain a Head or Tail if I throw a fair coin.

(b) I will grow wings by 6 p.m. today.

(c) I will get an even number if I throw a fair die.

2 A bag has 3 red, 4 green and 10 yellow beads in it. If Reece takes out a bead at random, what is the probability that it is:

(a) a red bead   (b) a green bead   (c) a red or green bead   (d) a pink bead
(e) a red, green or yellow bead.

3 The probability that somebody leaves a message on an answering machine is 0.32. What is the probability that they do not leave a message?

4 The probability that Vali misses the bus is $\frac{7}{15}$. What is the probability that she does not miss the bus?

5 Kelly says that when she spins the spinner, the probability that she gets a 4 is 1/3. Why is she wrong?

6 The probability that you pass a driving test on the first attempt is 0.35. If 200 people are taking their driving test, how many would you expect to pass first time?

> For Level 7 only

7 A fair die is thrown 600 times. If a five comes up 88 times what is the relative frequency?

8 A fair coin and a fair die are thrown together. Complete the sample space diagram below.

(a) What is the probability of getting a Head and a six?

(b) What is the probability of getting a Tail and an even number?

	1	2	3	4	5	6
Tail (T)					(T,5)	
Head (H)		(H,2)				(H,6)

9 Two fair die are thrown together and their totals multiplied. Complete the sample space diagram.

(a) What is the probability of a total of 12?

(b) What is the probability that the total is a multiple of 4?

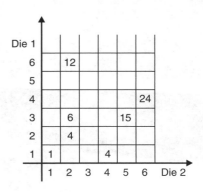

Answers

Number and algebra

Place value and the number system

1 $7\,°C$

2 $A = 15$ $B = 4$ $C = 4$ $D = -10$ $E = -10$ $F = -20$

3 (a) $x = 24$ (b) $y = 25$ (c) $z = 152$

4 19.4 kg, 19.04 kg, 6.302 kg, 6.032 kg, 2.74 kg, 2.7 kg

5 (a) $2 \times 2 \times 2 \times 2 \times 2$ (b) $7 \times 7 \times 7$ (c) $8 \times 8 \times 8 \times 8$

6 1.52×10^6

7 $\frac{6}{25}$

8 12%

9 (a) $0.\dot{7}$ 77.$\dot{7}$%   (b) $0.\dot{6}$ 66.$\dot{6}$%   (c) 0.6 60%   (d) 0.25 25%

10 6.49 (2 d.p.)

11 12.06 (2 d.p.)

12 9.5 (1 d.p.)

13 1200 (2 s.f.)

14 0.004 (1 s.f.)

Relationships between number and computation methods

1 (a) 20   (b) 26

2 (a) 11.73 (2 d.p.)   (b) 0.026 (3 d.p.)

3 (a) 3, 6, 9, 12   (b) 2, 3, 5, 7, 11   (c) 1, 2, 4, 5, 10

4 $2 \times 2 \times 2 \times 3 = 2^3 \times 3$

5 (a) 10   (b) 36   (c) 6   (d) 8

6 (a) 0.006   (b) 4   (c) 50 000

7 £12.24

8 13

9 38.7% (1 d.p.)

10 £25.50

11 15

12 £200 Ahmed, £300 Fiona

13 750 g

Solving numerical problems

1 25.50

2 £10.83

3 2.8

4 The tin which costs 48p, is the better value.

5 4 km/h

6 80.65 cm³ (2 d.p.)

7 45 minutes

Functional relationships

1 (a) $n + 6$ (b) $p - 4$ (c) $3y + 6$ (d) $\frac{h}{7}$ (e) $\frac{n}{p} - 5$

2 (a) 13.2   (b) −26   (c) −25.2

3 $4n - 2$

4 $2n^2$

5 A = (3, 2)   B = (1, 4)   C = (−2, 1)   D = (−5, 0)   E = (−3, −4)
F = (2, −2)

6 (a), (b) See figure

  (c) y = 4x is steeper
      than y = 2x.
      They both pass
      through the origin.

  (d) See figure

7 (a) 20 mph
  (b) Stationary, having a
      rest
  (c) 40 mph

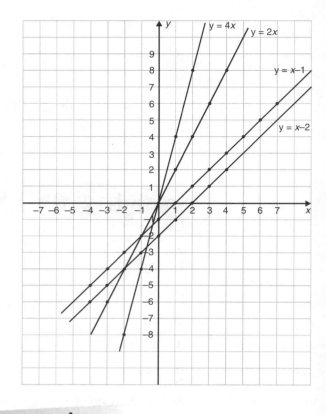

Equations and formulae

1 $S = 3P + 1$

2 (a) 10a   (b) 6a + 3b   (c) 5xy   (d) 10ab   (e) 12a²   (f) 6a + b

3 $8a + 10b + 5$

4 Card C

5 (a) a = 1   (b) n = 35   (c) n = 2   (d) n = 3   (e) n = −5   (f) n = −14

6 $x = −3, y = 4$

7 (a) $n < \frac{4}{3}$ (b) $n \leq 2$

Shape, space and measure

Properties of shapes

1

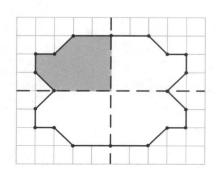

2 Hexagon

3

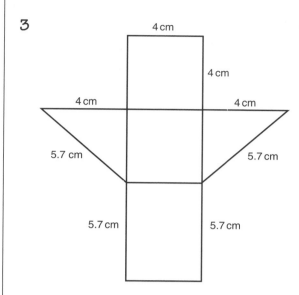

4 (a) a = 140°   (b) b = 80°, c = 80°, a = 100°   (c) x = 40°, y = 90°

(d) a = 50°, b = 130°, c = 50°, d = 50°

5 (a) Exterior = 60°   (b) Interior = 120°

6 (a) 13.8 m   (b) 13.3 m

7 94.3 km

Properties of position, movement and transformation

1 (a) 110°   (b) 240°   (c) 140°

2

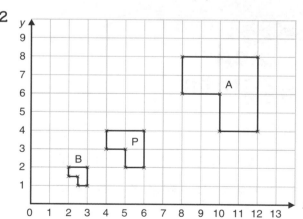

3 Forward 2. Turn right 90°. Forward 5. Turn right 90°. Forward 2. Turn right 90°. Forward 5

4

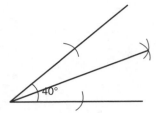

5

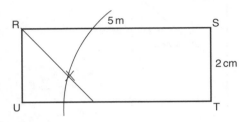

Measures

1 6.2 kg

2 42 mm

3 10.5 pints (approximately)

4 $6.25 \leq T < 6.35$

5 (a) 27 cm²   (b) 36 cm²   (c) 44 cm²   (d) 78.5 cm²

6 (a) 573.7 cm³   (b) 1534.7 cm³

7 30.8 cm (1 d.p.)

Handling data

Processing and interpreting data

1 (a) 480   (b) 360   (c) 600

2 (a) As the temperature increases more ice lollies are sold (positive correlation)

(b) As the temperature increases fewer cups of tea are sold (negative correlation)

3 (a)

Thumb length (cm)	Frequency
$2 \leq L < 4$	1
$4 \leq L < 6$	5
$6 \leq L < 8$	7
$8 \leq L < 10$	3
$10 \leq L < 12$	2

(b) 18   (c)

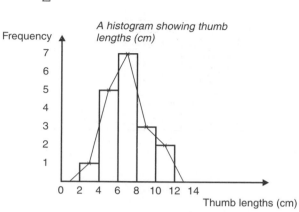

A histogram showing thumb lengths (cm)

4 Mean = 3.7 (1 d.p.), Median = 4, Mode = 5, Range = 6

5 (a) 7.7   (b) $5 \leq L < 10$

6 Your opinion that you want swimming lessons on a Saturday morning is evident

Estimating and calculating the possibilities of events

1

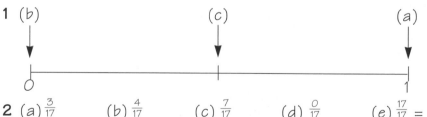

2 (a) $\frac{3}{17}$ (b) $\frac{4}{17}$ (c) $\frac{7}{17}$ (d) $\frac{0}{17}$ (e) $\frac{17}{17} = 1$

3 0.68

4 $\frac{8}{15}$

5 The outcomes are not equally likely, $p(4) = \frac{1}{2}$, as half of the spinner is a 4

6 70

7 $\frac{88}{600} = \frac{11}{75}$

8

Tail (T)	(T,1)	(T,2)	(T,3)	(T,4)	(T,5)	(T,6)
Head (H)	(H,1)	(H,2)	(H,3)	(H,4)	(H,4)	(H,6)
	1	2	3	4	5	6

(a) $\frac{1}{12}$ (b) $\frac{3}{12} = \frac{1}{4}$

9 (a) $\frac{4}{36} = \frac{1}{9}$ (b) $\frac{15}{36} = \frac{5}{12}$

Die 1

	1	2	3	4	5	6
6	6	12	18	24	30	36
5	5	10	15	20	25	30
4	4	8	12	16	20	24
3	3	6	9	12	15	18
2	2	4	6	8	10	12
1	1	2	3	4	5	6

1 2 3 4 5 6 Die 2